MACHINE
Quilting

A PRIMER OF TECHNIQUES

SUE NICKELS

American Quilter's Society

P. O. Box 3290 • Paducah, KY 42002-3290

www.AQSquilt.com

Located in Paducah, Kentucky, the American Quilter's Society (AQS) is dedicated to promoting the accomplishments of today's quilters. Through its publications and events, AQS strives to honor today's quiltmakers and their work and to inspire future creativity and innovation in quiltmaking.

EDITOR: SHELLEY HAWKINS
GRAPHIC DESIGN: AMY CHASE
COVER DESIGN: MICHAEL BUCKINGHAM
PHOTOGRAPHY: CHARLES R. LYNCH

Library of Congress Cataloging-in-Publication Data

Nickels, Sue.
   Machine quilting: a primer of techinques / Sue Nickels.
     p. cm.
     ISBN 1-57432-830-1
     1. Machine quilting 2. Machine quilting--Patterns.   I. Title.

     TT835.N493 2003
     746.46--dc22

                     2003017687
                     CIP

Additional copies of this book may be ordered from the American Quilter's Society, PO Box 3290, Paducah, KY 42002-3290, or online at www.AQSquilt.com.

DEDICATION

This book is dedicated to my mother and my mother-in-law.

In honor of my mother, Tiny Holly, for teaching me to love sewing and for being a wonderful and supportive mom!

In memory of my mother-in-law, Olga Nickels, who enjoyed patchwork quilting and was an enthusiastic supporter of my quilting endeavors.

Leatha (Tiny) Holly

Olga Nina Nickels
1922–2002

Acknowledgments

I would like to acknowledge the following people who have helped me throughout the process of writing this book. I could not have done it without their support.

To my editors, Barbara Smith and Shelley Hawkins, thank you for your confidence in my skills and your patience and guidance throughout the making of this book.

To the American Quilter's Society family, thank you for your continued support of quiltmakers and your appreciation of all the beautiful quilts in our world.

To Bernina of America, thank you for the generous use of my Bernina 170 QE sewing machine.

To Jane Garrison, thank you for all your kindness and continued support of my quilting and teaching.

To Jessi Nickels, thank you for helping your mom with this project and most especially for proofreading my manuscript.

To the following wonderful machine quilters who have allowed their quilts to be photographed for this book: Pat Holly, Gwen Marston, Caryl Bryer Fallert, and Melody Johnson. A special thanks to Pat Holly for the use of her antique quilts.

To my wonderful friends for helping to sew samples for the book: Nancy Chizek, Mary Ann Fielder, and Ruth LaCoe. Also, thanks to Sue Holdaway-Heys for lending me her MINI-FEATHER SAMPLER for the book.

To Helen Smith Stone, thank you for your long-arm machine quilting contribution.

To my family, thanks to Tim, Jessi, and Ashley for putting up with my deadlines. Also, thanks for your encouragement and support of my quilting career.

CONTENTS

Introduction 6

Machine Quilting History 9

Long-Arm Machine Quilting 12

Section One: Supplies 14

Sewing Machine	14	Marking Tools	22
Thread	15	Batting	22
Sewing Machine Needles	19	Basting Supplies	23
Miscellaneous Tools	21	Sewing Room	24

Section Two: Techniques 25

Straight-Line Machine Quilting 25
Free-Motion Machine Quilting 29
    Free-Motion Basics 31
    Stipple Quilting 34
    No-Mark Variations 36
    Straight Lines and Variations 37
Trace and Practice 38
    Marked Designs 53
    Feathers 57

Section Three: The Actual Quilt 67

Choosing Quilting Designs 67
Marking 75
Backing Fabric 76
Basting 77
Handling Bulk 79
Finishing 83

Section Four: Projects 88

Amish Bars 88
No-Mark Sampler 92
Feather Sampler 96
Patterns 100

Bibliography 109

Products 110

About the Author 111

Photo 1. JESSI'S BABY QUILT, 50" x 50", by Pat Holly, Muskegon, Michigan. This quilt was machine pieced, appliquéd, and quilted. It has cotton fabric and thread, and polyester batting.

Photo 2. WISHFUL THINKING, 71" x 71", by the author. A hand-pieced and hand-quilted quilt, started in 1985 and finished in 1987. This quilt has cotton fabric and polyester batting.

The quilting world has changed very much since I started quilting in 1978. One of the main changes has been the popularity and acceptance of machine quilting. Beginning as a hand quilter, I have a fondness for the beauty of this method and hope there will always be beautiful hand-quilted quilts. However, there is room in the quilt world for both hand and machine quilting. I hope to fit hand quilting into my life again in the future because of my love and appreciation of this time-honored tradition.

I also love and admire beautiful machine quilting. Because I was originally a sewing machine person, I was drawn to using the machine to make my quilts. If my grandmother and great-grandmother had had the sewing machines we have available today, I am sure they would be machine quilting.

Prior to becoming a quilter, I was a seamstress, having learned to sew at a young age. My mother's machine was almost always set up and my sister, Pat Holly, and I were encouraged to sew. We made doll clothes and then our own clothes throughout our childhood and teenage years. My high school graduation gift was my very own sewing machine.

After having my first daughter, I had a desire to learn how to quilt. I was inspired by a baby quilt my sister made for her new niece (photo 1). It was made the only way she knew how, completely by machine. When my daughter was six weeks old, I enrolled in a class at a local quilt shop and learned how to make quilts completely by hand, because machine techniques were not yet being taught (photo 2).

I still found time after having my second daughter to work on handmade quilts and joined a local quilt guild and a smaller quilt group. Gradually, machine piecing was being introduced to quilters. I loved the idea of piecing quilt tops with my sewing machine and soon had piles of tops that needed quilting.

While many of my friends sent their tops out to be hand quilted, I had a hard time justifying the expense as a stay-at-home mom. I continued to hand quilt and was not getting many quilts completed.

My sister took a machine quilting workshop by Harriet Hargrave and made a wonderful class sample. After seeing the sample, I realized my sewing machine could be used to quilt. Free-motion machine quilting allowed me to use the feather and cable designs I thought were only possible with hand quilting. Unfortunately, I did not have access to a workshop with Harriet and had to teach myself.

Practicing for six months, I felt confident enough to quilt a double-sized Nine-Patch charm quilt. Straight lines were quilted in the center pieced area, as well as a simple feather design on the border. That year, my guild sponsored a charm quilt challenge and show, so I entered my quilt. It was the first time anyone in my area had seen free-motion machine quilting. My friends wanted to know how it was done, so I began teaching machine quilting and have been teaching machine techniques ever since.

Machine quilting took a huge step forward when Caryl Bryer Fallert's CORONA II: SOLAR ECLIPSE (photo 3) won the Best of Show award at the 1989 American Quilter's Society (AQS) Quilt Show and Contest. It was the first time a machine-quilted quilt won a major award and it was controversial. Caryl was the perfect ambassador for machine quilting. Her quilt was exquisite and beautifully stitched. It deserved the honor and Caryl was a gracious winner, talking about her quilt to all and passing on her love for machine techniques.

Caryl won the AQS Best of Show award again in 1995 with MIGRATION #2, and in that amount of time, the controversy was over. A machine-quilted quilt could be appreciated and accepted for exceptional workmanship along with outstanding hand-quilted quilts. Today, many top awards go to machine-quilted quilts. In 1998, my sister, Pat Holly, and I won AQS Best of Show with a quilt that was made completely by machine. We heard so many wonderful comments from quilters around the country about the workmanship and the beautiful machine quilting.

Another reason machine quilting became more accepted during this time was because more quilters were trying it for themselves. You will appreciate machine quilting once you try it and discover the skill and talent required to do it beautifully. My original interest in machine quilting was to help me finish quilts faster. While it is faster than hand quilting for me, my first priority is to have a well-made quilt, and workmanship is not compromised for speed. Now, I choose to machine quilt because I love the way it looks and have spent up to 130 hours machine quilting one project. You can choose to stitch very simply and have a quick quilt with good workmanship, or you can stitch elaborately, spending many hours making an heirloom to be passed down through the years.

Photo 3. CORONA II: SOLAR ECLIPSE, 76" x 94", by Caryl Bryer Fallert, Oswego, Illinois. This was the first machine-quilted quilt to win the AQS Best of Show award in 1989. Hand-dyed and painted, 100 percent cotton fabric was used and the quilt was machine-pieced.

INTRODUCTION

The focus of this book is on the basics of machine quilting. My approach has worked well for me and the type of quilts I make. It is by no means the only way to approach machine quilting. My hope is that you will try the things I find successful, and if you like them, incorporate them into your machine quilting. The more ideas you are exposed to, the better you will be. Read many books and take a lot of workshops from local and national teachers. There will be some ideas you will use, others you won't. Machine quilting gives you room for choices.

The first section of the book is on supplies. Although this section is lengthy, it is important to understand the supplies you use, in addition to your supply choices. Next is the techniques section, which covers straight-line and free-motion machine quilting. No-mark designs, such as stipple quilting and its variations, are discussed, as well as motifs that need to be marked on the top, such as feathers, which is my favorite design. It is helpful to do the practice samples as you would if you were taking a class. The next section is about quilting the actual quilt. Marking, basting, and the important subject of how to handle the bulk are discussed. I have quilted small to very large projects with this approach and have been happy with the results. After completing the samples, try one of the projects in the fourth section to practice all aspects of machine quilting.

This book has the same format as my basic machine quilting workshop. I am confident that by the end of the book, you too will be able to successfully quilt all your projects. My goal is to take the fear out of machine quilting and for you to become confident in your ability to quilt any size or style of quilt. I hope you enjoy my approach and that it helps you on your quest to become the best quilter you can be.

Welcome to the wonderful world of machine quilting. Relax and have fun!

Sue Nickels

A few years ago, I heard the comment, "I hand quilt because it is the traditional way to quilt a quilt." It made me think about the traditions in quilting. I have always thought of myself as a traditional quilter and love old quilts. Most of my design inspiration comes from looking at antique quilts. Because of this, I researched the history of machine quilting and learned that it has existed since the sewing machine was first available to the home sewer.

My sister, Pat, and I collect antique quilts with visible machine stitching. They were hard to come by when we started our search. There wasn't much value placed on machine quilting in the 1970s and 1980s. When asked if they had any quilts with machine stitching, many antique dealers said they would not buy a machine-quilted quilt at auction because it was difficult to resell. As the popularity of machine quilting increased in the 1990s, we were able to find more and more antique examples. These quilts didn't suddenly materialize, because they had been there all along. Dealers recognized that they had value and others would buy them. We found some good deals early on, but the price has increased with popularity. The first quilts we found were machine quilted with straight lines in a grid across the entire surface. Referred to as mattress-pad quilting, this was an easy way for early quilters to approach machine quilting.

Understanding the history of the sewing machine has helped me appreciate these early machine-quilted quilts. The sewing machine was patented in 1846 by a New England mechanic named Elias Howe. Howe became ill and could not work, so his wife took in sewing to help with expenses. Howe saw the toll that handwork took on his wife and vowed to invent a machine to do the sewing. He was a brilliant mechanic but lacked the business skills to market his invention. In 1848, after returning from a sales trip to England, Howe learned that other men were selling sewing machines much like his own

Photo 1. The first Singer sewing machine, manufactured in 1851

invention. Howe and the sewing machine companies fought over the patent rights. The result was the first patent pool, called the Sewing Machine Combination, in which all parties of the lawsuit shared profits. Howe received $5.00 for every machine sold, and in the duration of his patent, he earned $2 million without ever manufacturing a machine.

Before the Civil War, most sewing machines were sold to factories. The Singer Company led the way in the home sewing market (photo 1). Isaac Singer was a savvy businessman. To combat the thinking of the times that a woman could not control machinery, he insisted that only young women demonstrate sewing machines in the showroom. Singer successfully proved that the sewing machine was easy to operate. The bigger problem was the cost of the machine. In today's terms, buying a sewing machine could be compared to purchasing a car without the ability to take out a loan. Because of this, many women shared their sewing machines. This practice did not stimulate sales. Being an astute businessman, Singer's partner, Edward Clark, developed a lease plan. A family could put $5.00 down and pay the rest in installments. Sales soared.

Even with the lease plan, owning a sewing machine was a status symbol. Many quilters wanted to machine quilt to show off their sewing machines. Although seamstresses found it difficult to control the layers of the quilt while treadling the machine, they did try. Once adept, some did machine quilt. An estimated 10 percent of quilts made from 1865–1900 had visible machine stitching. Most quilters stitched simple grids, as we found on many of the quilts we purchased from that era. Very few used the machine for extravagant stitching.

Photo 2. Quilted petticoat, ca. 1875, maker unknown, from Pat Holly's collection. This antique petticoat is machine-quilted.

We have found many examples of machine-quilted petticoats (photo 2). They were popular items to machine quilt because of their small, manageable size. Petticoats were quilted with more than just simple straight lines. Cables were a prevalent design on these undergarments.

Made in the 1870s, the RED-AND-WHITE QUILT (photo 3) is a wonderful example of machine

Photo 3. RED-AND-WHITE QUILT, 72" x 79", ca. 1870, maker unknown, from the author's collection. This is a beautiful example of straight- and free-motion machine quilting on an antique quilt. It has cotton fabric and batting.

Photo 4. FOUR-BLOCK APPLIQUÉ, 70" x 70", ca. 1890, maker unknown, from Pat Holly's collection. This is an unusual four-block design with primitive straight-line and free-motion quilting. It has cotton fabric and batting.

appliqué and quilting. It has straight lines sewn in the hanging-diamond pattern, as well as a nice free-motion design on the border. Another example of free-motion quilting is the FOUR-BLOCK APPLIQUÉ quilt (photo 4, page 10), dated around 1890. I believe the quilting was done in a quilt-as-you-go method. Quilters were creative with the sewing machine, even on these early quilts.

After the turn of the twentieth century, the return to hand work became the trend because it meant one had more leisure time. Most families could afford a sewing machine and it became less of a status symbol. Although there aren't as many examples of machine quilting during the early to mid-1900s, we have found a few. A fair amount of these quilts were quilted in the same straight-line grid, but we also found some wonderful free-motion work. An interesting example is the BLUE-AND-WHITE QUILT (photo 5) from the 1920s to 1930s era with an allover free-motion design, almost in long-arm machine style. The most beautiful example of machine quilting I found was on a yellow and purple DOUBLE WEDDING RING (photo 6) from the 1940s. It was free-motion

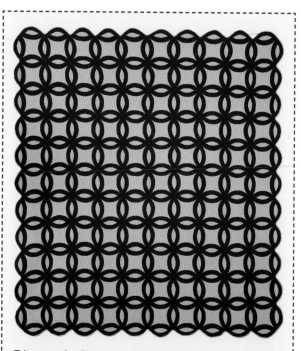

Photo 6. DOUBLE WEDDING RING, 79" x 73", ca. 1940, maker unknown, from the author's collection. This quilt is exquisitely free-motion machine quilted with motif designs and wavy lines. It has cotton fabric and batting.

quilted with a little wavy design along the rings and a curved motif in the crescent area.

There was a fair amount of straight-line machine quilting done throughout the first half of the twentieth century. I was delighted to see free-motion as part of this era and am still researching exactly how these early quilters achieved free-motion results, but there is no doubt in my mind they did. I have enjoyed researching machine quilting and the history of the sewing machine. It has happily confirmed that I am indeed part of the wonderful tradition of machine quilting.

Long-arm machine quilting has become another exciting addition to the quilt world. I have not used one of these machines but appreciate and admire all types of machine quilting. Many beautiful quilts with long-arm machine quilting have been at local and national shows over the past few years. The quilting contains far more than quick-and-easy repetitive shapes.

Photo 5. BLUE-AND-WHITE QUILT, 78" x 78", ca. 1920–1930, maker unknown, from Pat Holly's collection. This is a great example of free-motion machine quilting in an allover design. The quilt has cotton fabric and batting.

LONG-ARM MACHINE QUILTING

By Helen Smith Stone

Photo 1. **Long-Arm Machine**

Long-arm manufacturers rose to the call in the 1980s and upgraded their machines to meet the needs of modern quilters. Training workshops and conferences followed, some specifically designed for the long-arm quilter. Quilt show organizers added long-arm categories to their list of awards in judged exhibit competitions.

Designed to move over the quilt surface or sandwich, long-arm machines allow the operator to sew through the top, batting, and backing to create designs. The three layers are attached separately to the canvas rollers on the table for the long-arm machine, eliminating the need to baste as traditional quilters do.

The 1980s appear to be a time in our history for the acceptance of machine quilting. Before then, one often heard that it was not a true quilt unless it was hand quilted. During this time, quilting was evolving from needlework by hand to machine quilting, start to finish. While quilters were experimenting with machine quilting on their traditional home sewing machines, an alternative form with a larger, stand-up long-arm machine was growing in popularity (photo 1).

Quilters were looking for yet another way to finish their quilts, one that did not involve moving the quilt under the machine head. Many found the technique of moving the machine over the flat, stationary quilt appealing. Out of a desire to finish quilts faster, something interesting happened. Quilting entrepreneurs saw a small business opportunity in long-arm quilting. If space to house a machine and supplies is available, long-arm machine quilting can be enjoyable and profitable. It provides a service that many quiltmakers seek, especially those who prefer to piece and leave the quilting to someone else.

A versatile device, the long-arm machine is operated from the front or back of the head by holding the control handles and moving, or hand guiding, the head over the quilt in all directions as it sews. The controls for operating the machine are on the handles and range from a simple on-and-off switch to more elaborate features, such as a stitch regulator, bobbin-thread cutter, needle positioner, and more.

As previously mentioned, a long-arm machine requires some workspace. The machine head is mounted on a 12-to-14-foot-long table, which includes the rollers where the quilt layers are attached. The width of the table is generally about four feet. To operate efficiently, the quilter should be able to get around at least three sides of the table.

Standing and working from the back of the machine, the quilter is able to use special tools to quilt diagonals and circles for designs like cross-hatching or the Baptist Fan. This is also the position for quilting printed pantograph designs. These designs are traced with a laser light or metal stylus, a pencil-like attachment, while the machine sews them onto the quilt. Pantographs are available from several pattern designers and suppliers. This technique replaces the need to draw a stencil design on the quilt top and sew over it, as traditional machine quilters do. Some long-arm quilters use the stencil technique at times, however, depending on what they are creating.

The front of a long-arm machine is referred to as the freehand side. This position allows the quilter to get up close and personal with the quilt. While standing, or sitting on a tall stool, the operator hand guides the machine over the quilt surface, using the machine as a drawing pencil to create designs. This is the position for stipple quilting, meandering, or other background fillers. It allows a quilter to trace a design drawn on the fabric, or one that is applied through the use of tracing paper. The front of the machine facilitates the use of an expanded base and guides for straight-line, stitch-in-the-ditch quilting, or tracing acrylic templates.

Thread plays an important role in the long-arm quilting process, as with quilting on the home sewing machine. Most quilters purchase large cones containing 6,000 yards of thread, specifically designed for use on the long-arm machine. Keep in mind that these industrial machines operate at high speeds; therefore, the use of strong, high-quality thread gives better results.

Originally, cotton or cotton-wrapped polyester threads were the most popular choices of the long-arm quilter. Now, with more experimentation, a wide variety of threads is being used to enhance the beauty of the quilt. Smaller spools of specialty threads like metallic, rayon, and embroidery polyesters can be used effectively, especially with the addition of a small spool holder attachment. The tension may need adjustment to accommodate these threads successfully. Additional education in this area is well worth the investment.

Finally, don't be afraid to go beyond quilting quilts on a long-arm machine. You can quilt wearables, create chenille, baste quilts, do bobbin-thread drawing, and much more. You are limited only by your imagination, and remember, it really is a quilt when it's machine quilted, no matter what type of machine you use.

Helen Smith Stone (formerly Smith Prekker) is a long-arm machine representative, teacher, and show consultant to the quilting industry. She has been long-arm quilting for 10 years and lives in Duluth, Minnesota. For more information on long-arm machines, do an Internet search, keywords: long-arm quilting.

Supplies

Refer to the Products section, page 110, for a list of the products I prefer.

Sewing Machine

Any type of sewing machine can be used for quilting. Some machines make your job easier by having convenient features. Among these features are feed dogs with the ability to lower easily or be covered, a needle-down option, good foot pedal control of the machine's speed, and a large work table surface. Use the best machine you can afford. It is your essential tool for machine quilting and you should be comfortable with it. Keep your machine in good working order by having it cleaned regularly and oiled frequently.

Walking Foot

This important foot is used for straight-line quilting. It is also called an even-feed foot. Some machines have a built-in walking foot, but it is a separate attachment on most machines. This foot acts like a top set of feed dogs, feeding all three layers of the quilt through the machine evenly to prevent puckering and shifting of the layers. Make sure this foot is attached properly. The small fork needs to be placed around the screw that holds the needle in place. If it is not placed properly, the foot won't walk. For better visibility, an open-toe plate is available for some walking feet (fig. 1–1).

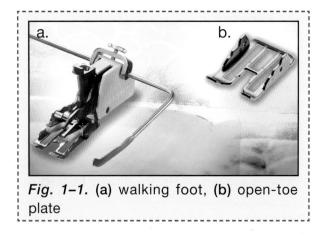

Fig. 1–1. **(a)** walking foot, **(b)** open-toe plate

Darning Foot

A darning foot is essential for free-motion quilting. For this technique, the feed dogs on the machine are lowered or covered. However, some quilters do free-motion quilting with the feed dogs engaged. The darning foot moves up and down slightly and allows the quilt to move freely while the foot keeps the surface smooth and flat. Free-motion quilting feels different from regular sewing and takes practice to achieve success. There are many different styles of darning feet, and each machine brand has its own specific foot. There are open- and closed-toe variations. They all do basically the same thing, yet some are easier to use than others because they provide better visibility. If you have choices in darning feet for your machine, try them all until you find one that gives you the best visibility and ability to control the quilt (fig. 1–2).

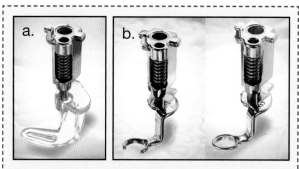

Fig. 1–2. **(a)** darning foot, **(b)** open-toe and closed-toe

Straight-Stitch Throat Plate

Today, sewing machines come with a throat plate that allows zigzag and decorative stitches. The plate is sometimes a large oval opening for the machine to do these stitches. When quilting, the layers of the quilt may get pushed down into the opening, and poor tension can be the result. By changing to a straight-stitch throat plate, which has a single hole for the opening, the quilt lies flat across the surface for a perfect stitch. Remember to do only straight stitching, no zigzag stitching, with this throat plate (fig. 1–3).

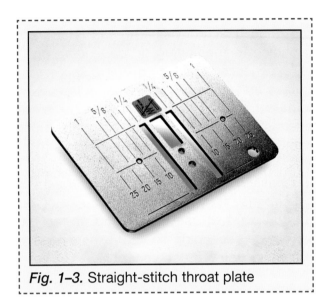

Fig. 1–3. Straight-stitch throat plate

Thread

Your choice of thread is important. Educate yourself on all the varieties and use only good quality thread. It makes a big difference in the success of your machine quilting. Cheap, poorly made thread causes problems such as frequent breaking, uneven tension, and skipped stitches. When students in my class have trouble with stitch quality, switching to good quality thread on the top and bobbin solves most problems without adjusting the tension or changing the needle.

Properly threading your machine is also important. A general rule is that cross-wound spools should be threaded on a horizontal spool pin, and straight-wound or stacked spools should be threaded on a vertical spool pin. The thread should always come off the spool easily and go through the tension bars evenly. Threads on big, heavy spools or on cone-shaped spools may need to be threaded off the machine using an auxiliary thread guide (see fig. 1–4, page 16) or a spool stand.

The type of thread you use determines the look you achieve on your quilt. Your experience level plays a part in your thread choice. A description of various types of threads follows, starting with the easiest thread to use as a beginning machine quilter.

Invisible Thread

This type of thread, also known as monofilament, comes in a few varieties. Invisible nylon thread, .004-weight, is usually on a cone-shaped spool. Invisible polyester thread is on a regular spool. When using this thread on the top of the machine, I use 50-weight, 100 percent cotton thread in the bobbin. Although some quilters use invisible thread in the bobbin with success, I prefer the look and feel of cotton thread on the back of the quilt. Invisible thread is heat sensitive. When ironing, turn the iron to a low setting and use a pressing cloth between the iron and the quilt. By following these guidelines, the thread has not melted on my quilts.

Invisible thread is helpful for beginning machine quilters if their free-motion stitches are uneven and inconsistent. It makes the stitches less noticeable, which can be a real asset to someone learning these techniques. I used invisible nylon thread on many of my early quilts and credit it for helping me become a successful machine quilter.

Starting as a hand quilter, I wanted to accomplish a hand-quilted quality on the machine. With invisible thread, this quality is achieved because the stitches are not highly visible and the thread is fine. I was resistant to machine quilting originally because, when using two strands of regular-weight thread, the quilt felt stiff. Combining invisible thread with regular thread in the bobbin provides a weight and feeling similar to hand quilting. Although it doesn't look exactly like hand stitches, it has that appearance. The highest compliment I have received was that my quilt looked hand-quilted. Invisible thread helped me become comfortable with machine quilting for those reasons.

Auxiliary Thread Guide

Threading the machine from a cone-shaped spool can be problematic. If threaded regularly from a vertical spool pin, the turning of the spool can cause the top tension to become tight. If threaded from a horizontal spool pin, the thread comes off fast and can tangle or break. To solve this problem, place the cone-shaped spool behind the machine and bring the thread through an auxiliary guide (fig. 1–4). This guide could be a safety pin taped upside down to the back of the machine or an empty bobbin placed on the spool pin. Pull the thread through the hole of the auxiliary device. When using fine invisible thread, you may need to loosen the top tension and make adjustments through the tension bars.

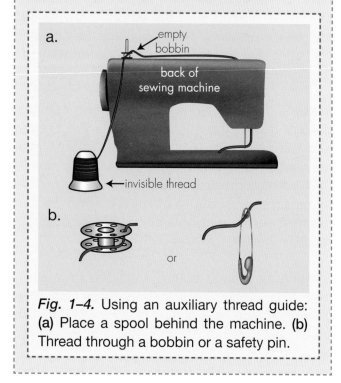

Fig. 1–4. Using an auxiliary thread guide: **(a)** Place a spool behind the machine. **(b)** Thread through a bobbin or a safety pin.

People have often asked about the longevity of invisible thread. Some of my quilts are 15 years old and have held up nicely; however, I carefully wash and store them. To investigate a longer amount of time, I have talked with quilt museum curators who collect contemporary quilts. They are documenting the quilts made with invisible thread and, over time, will be able to tell us what is hap-

pening. Some of them think the invisible thread will outlast the fibers of the cotton fabrics and may cut through the cotton fibers. Some quilters have expressed concern that invisible thread, like fishing line, will deteriorate over time. I have not seen these things happening on my quilts.

Using good quality invisible thread is an excellent choice for beginning or, depending on the quilt, experienced machine quilters. Another nice feature is that you can use the same thread over all different colors of fabric. I am happy to have used this thread early in my machine quilting career. Because its longevity is uncertain, I choose not to use invisible thread on heirlooms to be passed down through generations. The good news is that you can decide on which projects you want to use this thread. It can be a great choice depending on your experience level and the look you want on your quilt.

Cotton Thread

Becoming more comfortable with my machine quilting skills, I began to try other threads. I use 100 percent cotton fabrics for my quilts, and decided to try 100 percent cotton thread on the top and bobbin for quilting. There are many different weights and brands of cotton threads. Use a good quality thread that will look beautiful on the quilt's surface. I do not machine quilt with cotton thread designed for hand quilting. It has a waxed coating and can cause problems when used in the machine because it is less pliable.

Most cotton threads have some indication of the weight and ply. Thread weight, or denier, means fineness and is given in numbers. A higher number indicates a finer thread. Ply refers to the strand of thread. For example, three-ply has three strands of thread twisted together. This is my choice for quilting because it is strong. The thread I use for piecing is labeled 50/3, which means it is a 50-weight, 3-ply thread. Mercerized cotton threads are chemically treated to improve luster and strength. Some cotton threads are not mercerized and are softer with a matte finish. The weight and ply of the thread affects the look on the quilt surface. The following is a description of the varieties of cotton threads.

50-weight/3-ply thread. Choose a good quality cotton thread that closely matches the fabric you are quilting. As I became more comfortable with my quilting, I didn't mind that the thread was more visible. This thread is perfect for my traditional approach. The closer the thread matches the fabric, the less visible the stitches will be, which makes it suitable for the beginning machine quilter who does not want to use invisible thread. Some cotton threads are 50-weight/2-ply and are not quite as strong. However, they feel finer and can be a great choice.

40-weight/3-ply thread. Similar to a decorative thread, this thread is heavier and more visible on the quilt surface. It is a good choice as long as you know the look it will give on the quilt.

30-weight/3-ply thread. This heavier thread also gives a nice result. It is often referred to as machine embroidery thread and used for the heavier look of this technique. I treat this as a decorative thread because it is very visible on the quilt surface.

60-weight/2-ply thread. This is a fine embroidery-weight thread and can be used successfully for machine quilting. Its intended purpose is for machine embroidery techniques in the bobbin where the threads build up. The stitches are less visible because the thread is finer, making it a good choice for machine quilters. Because it is 2-ply, it is a weaker thread, so I quilt more heavily when using this thread and do not use it for machine piecing. I like this thread for machine stipple quilting, which is usually done around appliqué and quilting designs.

70- and 100-weight heirloom thread. Developed for heirloom sewing, these are very fine threads that can be used for heirloom machine quilting. They are a good substitute for invisible thread and blend nicely with the quilt fabric when used in a matching color.

Cotton-covered polyester thread. This is one of the most common sewing threads. It may not be the best choice for machine quilting because the quality can be unreliable.

Polyester Thread

There are many polyester threads available. Because cotton fabrics are mainly used in quilt-making, most quilters don't use polyester thread because they have been told to match the thread to the fabric. They may also have been told that polyester is stronger than cotton fabric and will cut through the fibers over time. However, this thread can be used successfully for machine quilting as long as it is good quality.

Silk Thread

Silk thread is a beautiful, lightweight yet strong thread that is great for machine quilting. One drawback is that it is expensive and hard to find in a variety of colors.

Decorative Thread

Decorative thread includes cotton thread in contrasting colors, variegated thread, variegated cotton thread, metallic thread, rayon thread, poly-neon thread, and acrylic thread. There are many others, with new thread becoming available all the time. To me, decorative thread is any highly visible thread that contrasts with the quilt fabric. To use decorative threads, you must be confident with your machine quilting skills and have good stitch control. As a beginner, it can be frustrating to use contrasting threads. As you become more experienced, this thread is fun and can give beautiful and unique results on your quilt (photo 1–1).

Photo 1–1. Detail of FEATHER/CABLE MINI SAMPLER with variegated thread

Decorative thread can be difficult to thread because of the variety of ways it is packaged on the spool. Find the best threading path by trying different options. If you have tension problems or thread breakage, try threading the spool differently. If you are threading on a vertical spool pin, try threading on a horizontal spool pin, or vice versa. If that doesn't work, try threading the spool off the machine through an auxiliary guide or spool stand (fig. 1–5). The threading path is the most important issue to resolve. Once the thread is feeding easily through the tension bars, most

problems are solved. After that, you may need to adjust tension for certain threads.

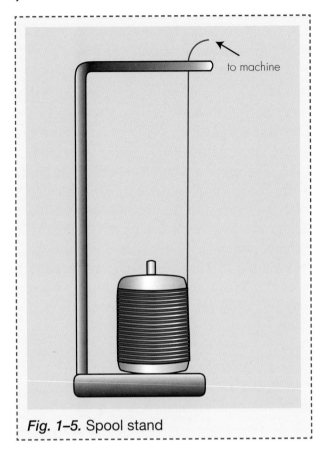

to machine

Fig. 1–5. Spool stand

Because of my traditional approach, I don't often use highly decorative thread on my quilts. I have used contrasting-colored cotton and variegated cotton threads. When using these as decorative threads, a 50-weight, 100 percent cotton thread of a similar color is used in my bobbin. There are many theories as to what bobbin thread is best with decorative threads. A fine, strong thread made particularly for use in the bobbin is popular with art quilters and those who do a lot of thread work on their quilts. Please refer to books and articles on this type of machine work for more suggestions.

When working with threads of different weights, you will need to experiment with adjusting tensions, top as well as bobbin. If you need to adjust the bobbin tension, I highly recommend using a second bobbin case. Leave your original bobbin case set at its manufacturer setting for best results in sewing with regular-weight threads.

Some threads don't have an indicated weight, so you have to do some detective work. I have learned to recognize the feel of a thread as compared to other threads. Because your choice of thread is so important, take the time to figure out the best one for the project. Remember to choose a good quality thread, whether it is invisible, cotton, polyester, or the many decorative threads available. Practice on a small sample using the fabric, batting, and threads for your project. This way you will see the results beforehand and be happy with the finished quilt.

Sewing Machine Needles

Choosing the right sewing machine needle is important. The best needle for a new project is a new needle. A needle should be changed after about eight hours of sewing. This may seem often; however, a dull needle or one with a burr causes many problems, such as skipped stitches and uneven tension. The following is a description of the parts of a sewing machine needle (fig. 1–6):

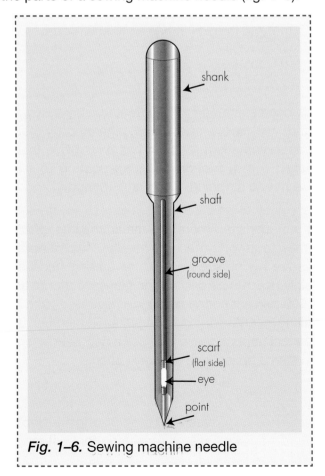

Fig. 1–6. Sewing machine needle

- Shank: the part of the needle that is inserted into the machine. Today's needles have a flat back, so they won't be inserted backward.

- Shaft: the body of the needle. The needle size is an indication of the shaft's thickness.

- Front Groove: this groove on the rounded side allows the thread to remain close as it travels down the needle.

- Scarf: the indentation at the back, or flat side, of the needle around the eye. A stitch is made as the bobbin shuttle swings into the scarf and hooks into the looped needle thread.

- Eye: the hole that the thread passes through. The size of the eye increases as the size of the needle increases.

- Point: the type of point is the main difference between needles. Select a point that works with the type of fabric you use.

The type of needle you use should match the fabric and the size of needle should match the thread and fabric. A fine thread in a large needle may cause the stitches to be made improperly. However, a thread too thick for the needle hole will fray and break.

The needle size refers to the shaft diameter. There are two sizing systems for needles. The European size is in hundredths of millimeters, ranging from 60–120. The American size is an arbitrary number, ranging from 8–21. The size is often listed for both systems, such as 70/10. The larger the number is, the larger the needle. The size I use depends on the weight of my thread. I use a size 80/12 needle with 50-weight, 100 percent cotton thread. Also, fine fabrics require small needles and heavy fabrics require large needles. For best results, use the finest needle that is small enough to pierce the fabric without leaving a hole. If skipped stitches occur, try the next larger needle.

The letter H appears on some needle packages, which stands for *Hohlkehle*, meaning long scarf in German. Long scarf needles are ideal for sewing zigzag stitches because the needle can get close to the shuttle and bobbin.

The following are the most common types of needles used by quilters. They are available in a variety of sizes. Use this information to help you decide which needle is best for your project. Schmetz is the most widely available brand of needle and that is what is described below, unless otherwise indicated.

Universal

This needle is called universal because it works on most fabrics. It works on woven fabrics as well as knits because the point is slightly rounded. Universal needles have a long scarf and an H code on the package. Many quilters use this needle because it is widely available.

Jeans/Denim

This needle is designed for sewing densely woven fabrics. It is a good choice for achieving perfectly straight stitches because it has a stiff, sharp point and a narrow eye. It is identified with a blue shaft and an H-J code. This a great needle for machine piecing and straight-line quilting because it makes a perfect straight stitch.

Microtex/Sharp

This needle has a thin shaft and slim, sharp point to achieve smooth stitches with lightweight woven fabric. It is identified with a violet band and an H-M code. This needle is used for heirloom sewing and is also popular for machine quilting.

Quilting

This needle has a thin, tapered, deep point for sewing multiple layers. It is identified with a green band and an H-Q code. It is an excellent choice for machine piecing and quilting.

Topstitch

This extra sharp needle has an eye twice as long as the universal needle and a deeper front. It is identified with an N code. This is a good needle to use with heavy or decorative threads.

Embroidery

This needle is designed for trouble-free sewing with machine embroidery and decorative threads. The eye is large enough to accommodate decorative threads and the front groove is deep enough to reduce skipped stitches. It is marked with a red band and an H-E code.

Metallica

This needle is used with metallic or flat filament threads. The eye is double the size in length, the front groove is deep, and the scarf is long. The eye has been treated to reduce the friction associated with metallic threads. It has an H-MET code.

Metafil by Lammertz

This needle is made from a treated alloy that withstands the high temperatures generated by metallic and synthetic threads. It has a long eye that is treated with a friction-reducing coating to minimize thread stripping. It has an H-M code.

As you can see, there are many choices when it comes to sewing machine needles. Microtex needles are my choice for machine quilting because I mainly use 100 percent cotton fabrics, cotton/blend, or 100 percent cotton battings. I have also used the quilting needle with good results. Remember that the most important rule is to use a new needle when you start a project and change it often.

Miscellaneous Tools
Curved-Point Scissors

These special scissors, or snippers, are great for cutting the thread ends at the surface of the quilt. Because they are curved, there is never a risk of clipping the fabric. The snippers are spring operated, which means you don't have to put your fingers in the holes of scissor handles. I also use the snippers for reverse sewing, or taking out stitches (fig. 1–7).

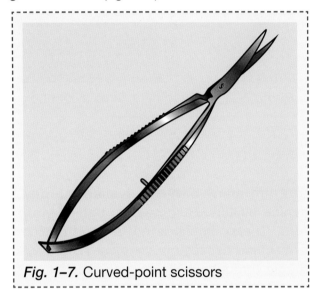

Fig. 1–7. Curved-point scissors

Self-Threading Needle

Easy to thread, this hand-sewing needle is used for easily burying threads between the layers of the quilt (fig. 1–8).

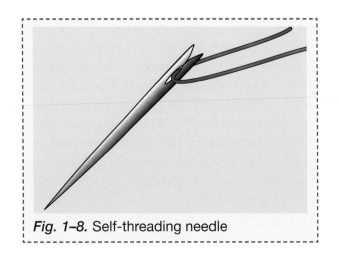

Fig. 1–8. Self-threading needle

Thread Stand and Auxiliary Guide

Use a thread stand for thread on cone-shaped spools or big, heavy spools that won't fit on horizontal or vertical spool pins. An auxiliary thread guide brings the thread from the spool stand to the exact point on the machine where it should be threaded. Some machines have auxiliary guides, but if yours does not, just use a safety pin taped upside down to the back of the machine or an empty bobbin on the spool pin, and thread through the small hole of each device (see fig. 1–4, page 16).

Rubber Glove Fingers

I started machine quilting long before there were products on the market specifically designed for the machine quilter. Right away, I realized it would be helpful to have something on my fingers to easily control and move the quilt when free-motion quilting. When I thought of using my rubber kitchen gloves, there was an immediate improvement in my ability to control the stitches. After about five minutes, my hands were sweating and it was uncomfortable. So I cut the fingers off the gloves, placed them on the first two fingers of each hand, and have used them ever since.

Now, there are many products on the market for this purpose, including secretary fingers, finger cots, gloves with rubber balls on them, rubber pads to place on the quilt, and hoops to place on the quilt. I have found that the rubber glove fingers give me the best traction, or grip, which is important in free-motion quilting. If you have a light touch on the quilt and can still move it easily, the result is smoother, more even stitches. When you don't have enough traction, the tendency is to push harder on the quilt, which results in jerky, uneven stitches.

Marking Tools
Pencils and Pens

When traditional machine quilting, it is sometimes necessary to mark the quilt top. It is important that the marking tool be easy to use. I use a soft, chalk-based silver marking pencil, which makes drawing on fabric easy. When drawing on the quilt, the pencil needs to mark easily without leaving a dark line and should be easy to remove. My silver pencil produces a nice line from a light touch and wears off easily. If a silver pencil does not show on your fabric, try a white one.

There are many other products on the market that can be used for marking quilt tops. They range from regular lead pencils to water-soluble pens. I recommend testing them carefully to make sure the marks come off easily. Do not iron your quilt top after marking with any pencil or pen because the heat may set the marks in the fabric and make them harder to remove.

Tracing Paper

Drawing quilting designs on tracing paper allows you to see how they will look on your quilt top. I lay the tracing paper over the quilt top and lightly draw my designs. Inexpensive rolls of tracing paper can be purchased at college book or art supply stores.

Light Box

A light box is helpful when marking quilting designs on dark fabric (photo 1–2). Inexpensive light boxes are available at quilt shops and craft supply stores. You can easily make your own light box by placing a light underneath the clear, acrylic extension table from your sewing machine. An old storm window that is supported on each corner can be used as well. A light box is a wonderful tool for quilting.

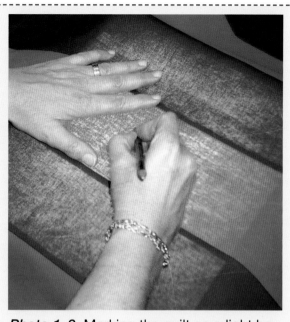
Photo 1–2. Marking the quilt on a light box

Batting

There are many battings available today for machine quilters. Buy the best batting you can afford. Cheap batting is not a good choice for the machine because it will most likely cause a struggle throughout the quilting process. When choosing batting, consider the look you want for your finished quilt, as well as the purpose of the quilt. I have always loved old quilts with cotton batting, and use cotton and cotton-blend battings mainly for this reason. Because these battings are flatter and have a slightly rough surface, they are easier to machine quilt than polyester batting, which slips more.

Open your batting and let it breathe before using it in your quilt. This allows any wrinkles and folds to relax before basting the quilt. It is a good idea to test battings with the fabric and threads you use. It is always good to know what the finished result of the batting will be before you baste and start quilting, only to realize you aren't happy with the look. Always read the instructions for your batting to know how far apart to quilt and whether it is recommended to pretreat or prewash.

Cotton Batting

Batting that is 100 percent cotton gives a flatter look to your quilt. It packages nicely and is easy to handle. It does not have much loft, however, and some quilters do not like it for this reason. This batting requires quilting closer together.

Cotton-Blend Batting

This batting is 80 percent cotton and 20 percent polyester. It is good choice for machine quilting because it is flat and easy to handle at the machine. The polyester makes the batting loftier and quilting designs show nicely. This is my favorite batting to use in traditional quilts. The brand I use recommends pretreating the batting before use because it may shrink when the quilt is washed. Refer to the instructions on the package for pretreating.

Polyester Batting

There are many kinds of polyester batting available. This batting has a loftier appearance than cotton battings, as well as a slippery surface. It needs to be basted more closely to keep it from shifting when quilting. It is harder to package at the sewing machine. Clips can be used to keep the quilt from unrolling. When used on dark fabrics, this batting may beard, which means polyester fibers migrate through the fabric. Dark polyester battings are available which hide this effect on dark fabrics.

Wool Batting

This batting is becoming popular for machine quilting. It looks and acts more like polyester batting when quilted and has more loft than cotton batting. It is also very warm when used in bed quilts.

Basting Supplies

An important step to successful machine quilting is to have a well-basted quilt. There are many options for basting. Take the time to do a good job,

whichever method you choose. I like to baste with safety pins and have found great success with this method. See page 77 for basting techniques. The following are supplies for the different methods.

Safety Pins

I use brass- or nickel-plated safety pins in size 0 or 1. Very small or very big safety pins can be harder to use. Baste about every 4" for cotton batting and about every 3" for polyester and wool battings. A large supply of safety pins is needed when working on large quilts. A safety pin closer is a great tool to help close the safety pins once they are inserted in the quilt layers.

Basting Spray Adhesive

This is a popular way to quickly baste a quilt. Follow the directions for the specific brand of spray adhesive you are using. It works well on small projects, but safety pins may be required in addition on larger projects to help secure the layers. The spray contains chemicals that are potentially harmful, so use it in a well-ventilated area.

Fusible Batting

These cotton and polyester battings can be steam ironed to successfully baste the layers of a quilt. Follow the directions for the specific brand you are using.

Basting Gun

To baste, this gun uses small tabs, similar to the plastic tabs that hold tags on clothing. The tabs are inserted through the quilt to secure the layers. These guns were popular a few years ago and some quilters still use them.

Thread

Thread is another basting option. This is not my favorite method because, when machine quilting, the darning foot gets caught on the thread. The basting threads are fussy to take out after the quilt is quilted.

Sewing Room

A well-planned sewing room is helpful for successful machine quilting. The following is a description of my sewing room, which hopefully will inspire you to set up your space for easier machine quilting.

My sewing machine is at table height, which means it is dropped down into the table. My extension table is the entire sewing table, allowing my quilt to be supported at all times without dragging or getting caught anywhere. A large surface for quilting is important. If you can't have a custom-made table, try finding a large, acrylic table that will fit your machine. It is well worth the investment. My sewing table is deep behind my machine. As the bulk of the quilt moves behind the sewing machine, it doesn't drop off the table or stop at a wall. My table is about 6 feet deep and 3½ feet wide. The sewing machine is at the very front and slightly to the right of the table because more room is needed on the left side to support the bulk of the quilt.

Behind my chair, there is an ironing board used to support the bulk over my shoulder when working at the front of the quilt (fig. 1–9). I never support the quilt with my body, which eliminates a sore back and shoulders, even when working on very large projects. I use a secretary's chair that allows me to easily adjust the height to sit in the perfect position at the machine and rest my hands flat on the quilt. With shoulders relaxed, the area from your fingers on the quilt to your bent elbow should be parallel to the floor. Scrunched shoulders cause neck and shoulder stiffness. Sitting straight in my chair allows me to be as close to my machine as possible.

Good lighting is an important consideration. If you can't see what you are quilting, you can't quilt very well. I have overhead lighting from different places

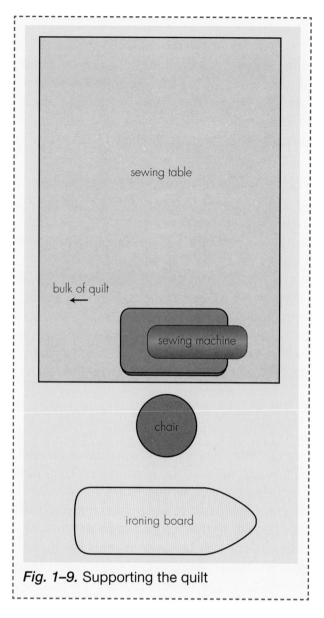

Fig. 1–9. Supporting the quilt

so shadows don't appear on my quilt. An adjustable lamp is in front of my sewing machine so the area I am quilting is well lit.

If you can't redesign your sewing room right away, you can always find ways to make it work better by improvising. When I started machine quilting, I had to be creative. My sewing machine was placed at the long end of my dining room table, so the surface around the machine needed to be larger. I used old phone books to make an extension table. Sitting on about three pillows to reach the right height, I used a floor lamp over my shoulder to see well. I am much happier now with a customized sewing area, but I still made some pretty nice quilts when improvising.

This section explores the two types of machine quilting: straight-line and free-motion. It is helpful to work on the practice samples after reading this section completely.

Straight-Line Machine Quilting

This is the easiest type of machine quilting and a good place to begin. You can quilt the entire surface with simple, straight lines in a grid or hanging diamonds. This was done on many old quilts because it was a quick and easy way to finish. Gwen Marston's HOUSES AND STARS (photo 2–1) is an example of machine quilting done today in the style of our great-grandmothers. Gwen quilted a straight-line grid with cotton thread across the entire surface.

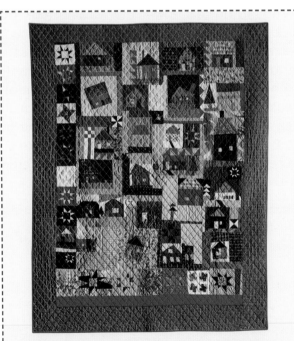

Photo 2–1. HOUSES AND STARS, 56" x 70", by Gwen Marston, Beaver Island, Michigan. The blocks were pieced by Gwen and students at the Beaver Island Quilt Retreat. Gwen straight-line machine quilted in an early style. Cotton fabrics and batting were used. Photo by Keva Partnership.

Straight lines can be combined with some free-motion quilting for a nice look. I sometimes use diagonal lines on borders and surrounding appliqué. I mainly use straight-line quilting to secure the quilt by stitching in the ditch along the rows of piecing or appliqué. However you decide to use straight lines, it is important to know how to do them properly. I sew straight lines with the walking foot. Even though my quilt is well or securely basted, it is nice to have the added security of straight lines.

Practice Sample

Prepare a 10" square package of two pieces of muslin and one piece of cotton batting. Mark a 1" grid on the muslin, leaving a 1" border around the edge (fig. 2–1, page 26). Safety pin baste to hold the layers together (photo 2–2).

Photo 2–2. Straight-line practice sample, finished with binding

Please note that on my square practice samples, I have used solid fabric in a variety of colors to have a more colorful book. In the description of the quilt packages, muslin is used because it is usually the least expensive fabric for practicing. You could use any solid-colored fabric in your stash, if desired.

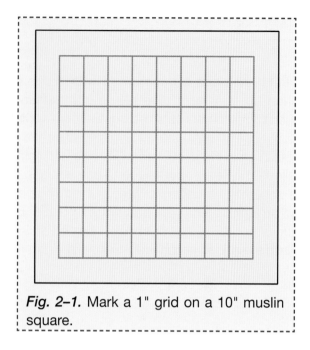

Fig. 2–1. Mark a 1" grid on a 10" muslin square.

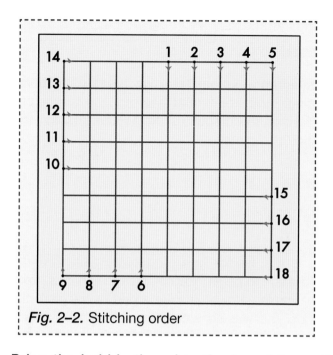

Fig. 2–2. Stitching order

Thread the machine with invisible thread on the top and 50-weight cotton in the bobbin. Refer to page 16 in the Supplies section for instructions on threading invisible thread. Set the machine on a straight stitch. Use of a straight-stitch throat plate is optional. Attach the walking foot securely to the machine, referring to page 14 in the Supplies section for instructions. Feed dogs should remain engaged; do not lower them for straight-line machine quilting with the walking foot. If you don't have a walking foot, use a regular presser foot. This is a good practice piece to see how your machine handles the layers without a walking foot. In my experience, if you do much machine quilting, it is helpful to have a walking-foot attachment.

Treat the practice squares as quilts. Plan your sewing path before you start quilting. Always start at the centermost grid line on the top and sew the entire line. Then move to the right and sew the next row, and so on. Turn the sample upside down, 180 degrees, and work again from the center of the square to the right. Repeat this until the square is finished (fig. 2–2). This method on handling the bulk of the quilt is described thoroughly in Section Three. It is important to consider bulk and how to handle it from the beginning.

Bring the bobbin thread to the top of the quilt before you begin quilting. I like to know where my bobbin thread is all the time to keep it from getting sewn into the back or becoming tangled as I start sewing. To do this, lower the walking foot. Hold the top thread as you take one stitch, moving the needle down and up, to bring the bobbin thread to the top of the quilt. Lift the foot after taking this stitch and pull on the top thread. The bobbin thread should come up as a little loop. Pull on it to bring it all the way through to the top of the quilt (fig. 2–3). If you have trouble with this, make sure the needle is in its most upright position after taking the stitch. Also make sure you only took one

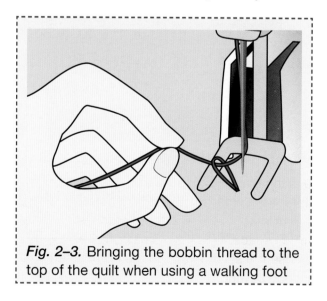

Fig. 2–3. Bringing the bobbin thread to the top of the quilt when using a walking foot

stitch with the needle down into the quilt one time and back up. Sometimes, the invisible thread on the top keeps pulling and the bobbin thread won't come up. If this happens, just pull on either side of the stitch to force the bobbin thread up.

Securing stitches when starting and stopping is necessary when machine quilting. Position the walking foot so the needle is back in the same spot the first stitch was taken. Lower the walking foot. Holding both the top and bobbin thread, make 8 to 12 small stitches (fig. 2–4). Do not sew in the same place, overlapping stitches. This creates a ball of bobbin thread on the back of the quilt, and once the ball is cut off, the threads are not secure anymore. Because you are practicing securing threads on this sample, the grid is marked 1" away from the edges. If starting at the edge of the square, you would not need to secure the threads. The binding in an actual quilt would secure those threads.

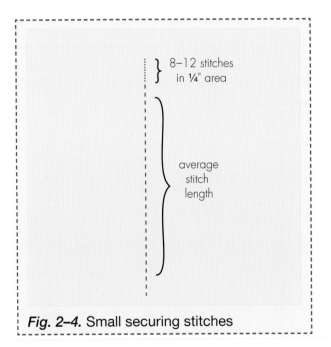

Fig. 2–4. Small securing stitches

One way to make the securing stitches is to lower the stitch length to a .5 setting. Every machine has different settings, so you need to find the best one for your machine. The 8 to 12 stitches need to be in a ¼" space. Once the small stitches are made, increase the stitch length to the normal setting and continue sewing.

Another option is to keep your stitch length at the normal setting and hold back on the quilt so it can't progress as quickly, manually taking the small stitches. Once you have the 8 to 12 stitches, release the quilt and continue with the normal stitch length. Some machines don't respond well to this. If the machine jams at all, do not use this method. It is harder to control the amount of stitches with this method, but once you get control, it works well.

If your machine has memory when moving between stitches, this provides another way to make the small stitches. With the straight stitch on the normal setting, go to the zigzag stitch and set the width to zero. You now have another straight stitch. Adjust the stitch length to the small stitches. Once you have made these stitches, go back to the normal straight-stitch setting. Move back and forth between these two stitches as needed.

For a normal stitch length, I use a setting of 2.0, which is about 12 to 14 stitches per inch. This length may be a little small for some quilters. I like it because my free-motion stitches are on the small side, and this keeps my stitch length consistent throughout the quilt. A setting of 2.5, which is about 10 to 12 stitches per inch, is also good. The stitches shouldn't be too large, such as 6 to 8 per inch, or too small, such as 16 to 18 per inch. There is room for personal preference. The most important criterion is to have consistent stitch length throughout the quilt.

Continue sewing the grid line with the normal stitch length and follow the line carefully. When far enough away from the start, clip the top and bobbin threads right at the surface of the quilt. At the end of the line, secure your stitches again by making 8 to 12 small stitches. Clip the top thread, then lift the quilt and carefully clip the bobbin thread with the curved snippers (fig. 2–5, page 28). By doing this, you don't have to bring the bobbin thread to the top once the small stitches have been made. When you are about 1" to 2" away from the safety pins, remove them so they are not in the way of stitching. It becomes harder to remove them if you are too close.

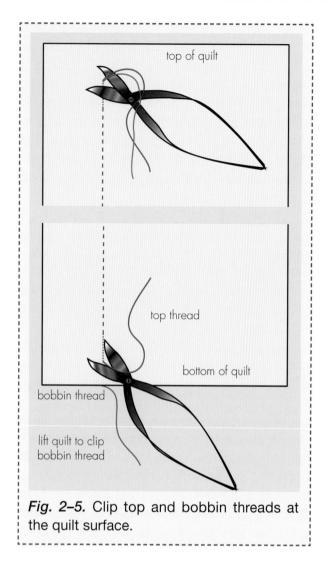

Fig. 2–5. Clip top and bobbin threads at the quilt surface.

Is the sample well basted? If not, there might be shifting problems. Some sewing machine manufacturers suggest that you have a little fullness in front of the walking foot for it to do the job properly. Try this to see if it helps; however, I don't do this on my machine and I still get good results.

Once you are done with this sample, you should feel comfortable with straight-line machine quilting. Try another practice sample with a 50-weight cotton thread on the top and in the bobbin to see how you like the look compared to invisible thread (photo 2–3). Also, try some decorative thread on this second sample. When making the securing stitches with 50-weight cotton thread, follow the same method used for invisible thread. When using decorative thread, you may need to be more careful. With some decorative threads, such as metallic, rayon, and heavier cotton threads, clipping at the surface of the quilt may cause fraying. With these threads, make the small securing stitches, but leave an approximate 6" tail. Pop these threads onto a self-threading needle, then bury the thread ends in the batting. The small stitches secure the threads, but you want to bury the ends to avoid fraying.

Complete the sewing on your sample to become comfortable with securing the stitches and straight-line stitching. The following are some things to look for as you sew.

Adjust the top tension, if necessary, when sewing with invisible thread. If you see bobbin threads showing on the top, you need to loosen the top tension. For example, if the top tension is set at 5, turn it to 4. Sew another line, and if bobbin threads still show, loosen the top tension to 3, and so on. Also, make sure you are threading the invisible thread properly and that the threading path is good.

If the layers shift, make sure the walking foot is on correctly. If you can, adjust the presser foot pressure and see if the layers move more evenly.

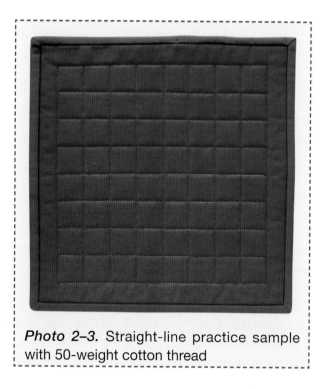

Photo 2–3. Straight-line practice sample with 50-weight cotton thread

Stitching in the Ditch

Stitching in the ditch accomplishes securing straight lines on a quilt and is not highly visible. When stitching in the ditch, sew on the lower side of the seam. When seam allowances are pressed in one direction or the other, sew on the side that does not have the seam allowances (fig. 2–6). This way, you are sewing right next to the piecing stitch, not exactly on it. The high side with the seams almost covers this stitching. On a pieced quilt, you may have to switch from one side of the seam to the other along one row of stitches. If you sew on

the side with seam allowances, it is more visible and looks like topstitching.

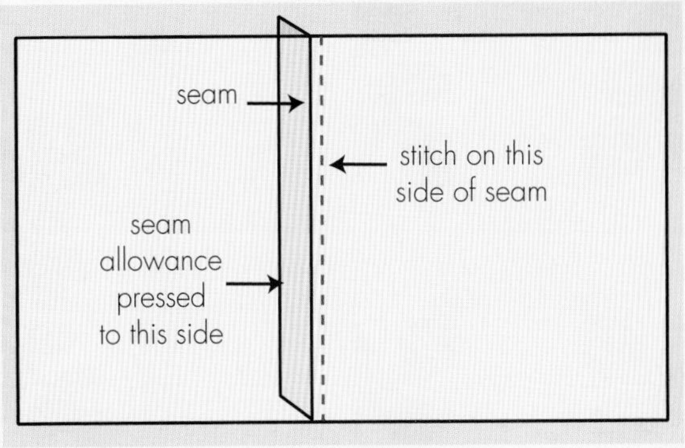

Fig. 2–6. Stitching in the ditch

Do all of your straight stitching first, then switch to free-motion quilting. A further discussion of the stitching order is in Section Three, page 80. It is a good idea to make a small package of the fabrics and batting used in your quilt. Thread the machine with the top and bobbin thread you will be using and practice a few rows of straight stitching before starting on the actual quilt. You can discover tension and threading problems, or just make sure you like your thread choices. All the straight stitching can be done with the walking foot.

Free-Motion Machine Quilting

Here is where the real fun begins. I love free-motion quilting and know you will too. It allows you to create curved designs with the sewing machine. We will start with stipple quilting and some variations, then explore free-motion quilting with designs marked on the quilt top. This enables you to do all those wonderful quilting designs like cables and feathers (photo 2–4, page 30). You are encouraged to do the practice samples. They provide a good understanding of these concepts.

If you have not done free-motion quilting before, it is an unusual way of sewing on the machine. It takes practice and patience to achieve smooth, even

stitches. Keep in mind the importance of thread choices. A beginner should use invisible thread or matching cotton thread. If you have some experience with machine quilting, use this information as a guide to help you improve what you already know. The more you know about free-motion machine quilting, the better machine quilter you will be.

Practice Sample

Prepare a 10" square package of two pieces of muslin and one piece of cotton batting. Mark a straight line through the center of one muslin square in both directions to make four quadrants. Safety pin baste the layers (photo 2–5, page 30).

Thread the machine with invisible thread or matching 50-weight cotton thread in the top and matching 50-weight cotton thread in the bobbin. Use the straight-stitch setting, and if available, a straight-stitch throat plate. Place the darning foot on the machine and lower the feed dogs. Some machines have a cover plate that covers the feed dogs. Use the needle-down option if available. I use rubber glove fingers on the first two fingers of each hand when free-motion quilting. Some quilters like to use the thumbs as well.

Stitch-length control is gone once the feed dogs are lowered. This is a hard concept to grasp at

Photo 2-4. SEPTEMBER BUD AND ROSE, 47" x 47", by the author. A good example of traditional free-motion quilted feathers. Cotton fabric and threads and cotton-blend batting were used.

Photo 2-5. Free-motion practice sample, finished with binding

first. If you don't move the quilt, it will stay in place and you will get overlapped stitches. To make the small stitches, move the quilt very slowly. The slower it is moved, the smaller the stitches, and the faster it is moved, the bigger the stitches. The other factor that determines stitch length is the speed your machine is sewing. If your sewing is extremely slow, it can be hard to get smooth, even stitches. Sewing at a medium to medium-high speed makes it easier to achieve consistent stitch length. Stitch length is ultimately determined by the relationship between the speed of the machine and the how fast you move the quilt.

Start with some warm-up exercises on the practice sample to get a feel for free-motion quilting. Always treat the practice samples as if they were quilts and think about the bulk moving to the left. There are different designs for each quadrant of this sample.

In the first quadrant, sew some wavy lines in rows across the surface, beginning and ending each line with 8 to 12 small stitches (refer to figure 2–9, page 33). Start at the top of the quadrant. Lower the darning foot. Holding the top thread, take one stitch, moving the needle down and up. Lift the darning foot and bring the bobbin thread to the top of the quilt. Both threads should be under the darning foot (fig. 2–7). Position the darning foot so the needle starts in same hole as the bobbin thread. Lower the darning foot, hold both threads with a little tension, and begin moving the quilt slowly to make 8 to 12 small stitches.

Continue stitching, moving the quilt faster to make normal-length stitches. Remove the safety pins when you are about 1" to 2" away from them. When you are far enough away from the start, stop sewing with the needle down and clip the threads at the surface. Carefully start sewing again. Slow the movement of the quilt to make the small stitches at the end. Clip the top thread

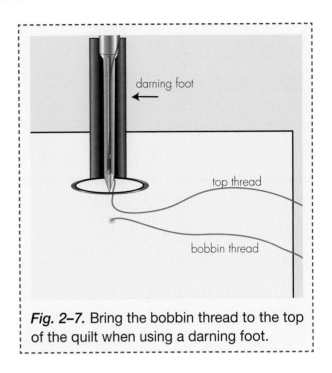

Fig. 2–7. Bring the bobbin thread to the top of the quilt when using a darning foot.

at the surface and lift the quilt to carefully clip the bobbin thread. To make another wavy line, start back at the center of the quadrant, securing the stitches at the start and stop. Refer to the following sidebar on free-motion basics, and practice the wavy lines with these concepts in mind.

Free-Motion Basics
Smooth, Consistent Stitches

The most important part of free-motion quilting is achieving smooth, consistent stitches throughout. To do this, you must be able to move the quilt easily with the help of rubber glove fingers or other tools. It is also important that the quilt does not get caught or drag anywhere. You will eventually be in tune with the motor speed of your machine and the speed at which you need to move your quilt. They need to work together for success. It's like rubbing your tummy and patting your head – it takes some concentration.

I like to sew at a medium to medium-high speed. If you are able to move the quilt fairly easily and quickly, sew at a medium speed to match. If you need to move the quilt a little slower, when following marked lines on the quilt for example, slow the machine speed to match. I rarely sew at high or low speed. It is easy to adjust the speed of the machine with a good foot-control pedal, so move the quilt at the appropriate speed for your project, then adjust the speed of the machine to match.

Finger Placement

Always keep your fingers on the quilt surface while sewing. This means that when you need to reposition your hands, stop sewing with the needle down, reposition, and start sewing again. If you move your hands while sewing, you lose control of the quilt. A small practice piece will stay in the same place if your hands

Free-Motion Basics (continued)

aren't guiding it. This can cause overlapped stitches and thread buildup on the back of the quilt. On a large project, the quilt is usually touching you over the shoulder or resting on your chest. When you lift your hands off the quilt while sewing, you are always moving and the quilt will too. The results are jerky, uneven stitches until your hands are on the quilt to direct it.

If the needle is down while you position your hands, the quilt will stay in place. If your machine does not have a needle-down option, which means the needle stays in the quilt every time you stop sewing, just leave your left hand on the quilt so it won't move and manually put the needle down with your right hand. Then reposition both hands and start sewing again, making one stitch in the same hole you stopped. This first stitch can be awkward and uneven, but this method will help you realign. Stopping to reposition my hands has become so ingrained that I can't sew if my hands are off the quilt.

Hand Placement

If looking at a clock, the nine and three positions are a good placement for your hands on the quilt. Stay about 1" to 2" away from the needle (fig. 2–8). As you move out of this area, you lose much of your ability to get smooth, controlled stitches. I can travel to about ten and two on the clock, then start to lose control of the quilt and need to reposition my hands.

On big quilts, I am always working as if there is only a 10" square area and reposition my hands often. Moving the quilt package sideways or twisting it to make the stitches will cause you to lose control. Try to do all your

stitching right to left and up and down in this 8" to 10" area. Another helpful concept is one that artists use when drawing and painting. Use your hands and arms, not just your fingers, to make movements. You will have better control if your whole arm is working with you.

Stitching Order

It is easier working from the top of a quilt to the bottom. With free-motion quilting, you have the ability to go backward, meaning you can move the quilt toward your body. With this method, you are not directionally challenged as in regular sewing with the feed dogs engaged. Although the quilt can be moved in any direction to sew, it is easier to see where to stitch if the quilt is moved away from you. When you move it toward you, the stitches are made behind the darning foot attachment, making them difficult to see. I sew backward when necessary, but it was hard to do at first.

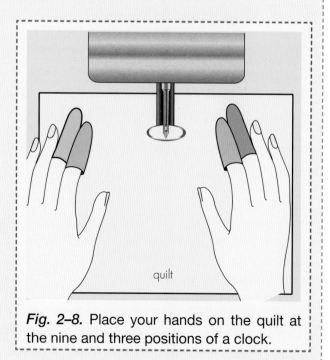

Fig. 2–8. Place your hands on the quilt at the nine and three positions of a clock.

In the second quadrant, try sewing some simple loops. Remember to secure both the starting and stopping stitches, even though this is a practice sample. It is important that these small stitches become ingrained. In the next quadrant, try writing your name in cursive. Your stitches should be more even and consistent as you have become more familiar with moving the quilt. If they aren't, think about some of the free-motion basics and apply them if you have not already done so. In the last quadrant, repeat the wavy lines, loops, and writing (fig. 2–9).

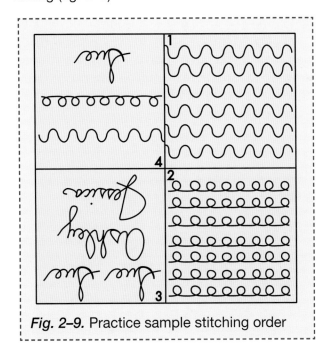

Fig. 2–9. Practice sample stitching order

One last thing to check on this sample is stitch quality. Look at the front and back of the sample to see that the tensions are properly adjusted. If the bobbin thread shows on the top of the quilt, lower the top tension. Sew another row to see if there is an improvement, and lower the tension a little more if not. If top thread is showing on the back of the quilt, tightening the top tension is usually enough for the stitches to look good.

You may need to adjust bobbin tension, especially if using decorative threads. Purchase a separate bobbin case to do this and keep the original case at the manufacturer setting for regular sewing. Find the screw on the bobbin case that adjusts tension. If looking at a clock and the screw's position is 12, tighten the tension by turning the screw to the right. To loosen the tension, turn the screw to the left. Small turns are all that's required. Turn the screw a quarter turn at a time and see if it has helped (fig. 2–10). Remember where the screw was originally and return to that spot when done sewing with a particular thread combination.

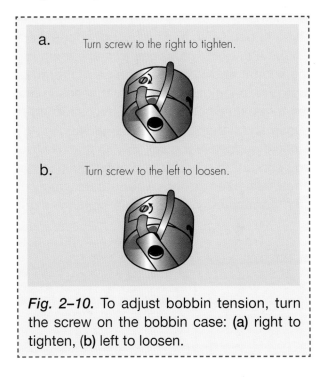

a. Turn screw to the right to tighten.

b. Turn screw to the left to loosen.

Fig. 2–10. To adjust bobbin tension, turn the screw on the bobbin case: **(a)** right to tighten, **(b)** left to loosen.

Stitch quality is also affected by the throat plate. Use a straight-stitch throat plate on your machine if possible. If you don't have one, the bobbin thread on the back of the quilt may have a very flat appearance. This look is more visible when quilting circles and loops. It means the quilt is being pushed into the large zigzag opening and the stitch is being made improperly. With a straight-stitch throat plate, the quilt will lie flat, allowing a more perfect stitch to be made. You can adjust tension to help solve this, but it is best to use a straight-stitch throat plate. If you have followed this advice and still have trouble, consider some of the recommendations given in the Supplies section. Use good quality thread, as well as a new and appropriate needle, and have your machine cleaned and oiled. You have made a great start with free-motion quilting and are on your way to more fun.

Stipple Quilting

Stipple quilting has become popular and most quilters want to learn to how do this technique because it is relatively easy. I like to traditional stipple quilt similar to the hand stippling on antique quilts (photo 2–6). Stipple stitching consisted of very small curvy shapes that didn't cross over themselves. It was used for heavily quilting an area to condense it. It was usually done around appliqué and quilting designs to make them more dimensional and visible. Machine quilters have adapted it to look like little puzzle pieces in many sizes to create different looks. Small stippling has a dense and flat appearance. Large stippling over the entire surface is a quick way to machine quilt. Traditional stipple and free-motion quilting have sometimes been grouped together, which can cause confusion. When stipple quilting, I don't cross over my lines, but do so all the time for free-motion quilting and get fabulous designs.

Try to sew these puzzle-piece shapes randomly, not forming a repetitive pattern. Also try to keep the pieces about the same size throughout the project. Determine a path by using your finger to trace the area before starting. Stipple quilting is a lot like handwriting. Yours may look different from mine, but it doesn't make one right or wrong. It should cover the area evenly and not cross over the lines of the previous stitching – other than that, just have fun and play. There are stipple stencils and patterns available, which makes this a design you have to follow and stay on the lines. Try to do it without marking any lines. If you have trouble making the shapes, try drawing them on your practice sample or drawing them on a piece of paper first. Sometimes you just need to visualize it before you can quilt it.

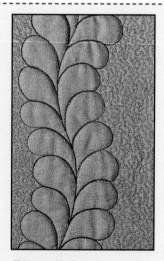

Photo 2–6.
FEATHER/CABLE MINI SAMPLER, 18" x 18", by the author. This quilt has traditional stipple quilting throughout the background. A whole-cloth stencil was used for the designs. See Products, page 110. Cotton fabric, thread, and cotton-blend batting were used.

Practice Sample

Prepare a 14" square package of two pieces of muslin and one piece of cotton batting. Mark a straight line through the center of one muslin square in both directions to make four separate quadrants. Safety pin baste (photo 2–7).

Photo 2–7. Stipple practice sample, finished with binding

Thread the machine the same as for free-motion quilting, page 29. You will use different weights of thread to show how it affects the look on the quilt. The machine setup is also the same as for free-motion quilting. Follow the instructions from the free-motion sample, such as securing starting and stopping stitches, stopping with the needle down to reposition your hands, and coordinating the speed you move the quilt with the sewing machine speed.

Refer to the Trace and Practice section, pages 38–41, and practice stipple quilting on the sample. In the first two quadrants, use 50-weight, 100 percent cotton thread. I have used 50/3-ply cotton thread successfully for medium to large stipple quilting. For small and tiny stipple quilting, I have used 60/2-ply cotton thread and fine heirloom thread to achieve a more subtle look. Invisible thread blends in the best (photo 2–8).

I hope traditional stipple quilting has become easier after sewing this sample. It can sometimes become easier after learning more free-motion forms, so come back to it a little later if you struggled and try again. I promise it will be easier.

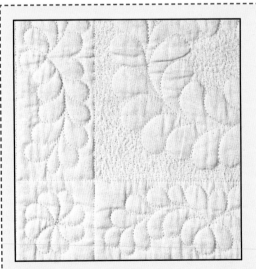

Photo 2–8. MINI-FEATHER SAMPLER, 18" x 18", by the author, from the collection of Sue Holdaway-Heys. This quilt has very small traditional stipple quilting. Cotton fabric, thread, and cotton-blend batting were used.

No-Mark Variations

There are many varieties of free-motion quilting for background and allover designs. It is nice to use designs that don't need to be marked on the quilt. In the following exercises, you will almost be drawing on the quilt with the machine. You will explore crossing over lines and much more – the options are limitless! I am going to give you some ideas, but feel free to develop your own designs too. With all these designs, the basic concepts from the previous techniques still apply. Fill in the areas evenly. This subject is discussed more thoroughly in Section Three.

Practice Samples

Prepare two 14" square packages of two pieces of muslin and one piece of cotton batting each. Mark a straight line through the center of the top muslin square in both directions to make four areas to sew for each package. Safety pin baste to hold layers together (photos 2–9 and 2–10).

Photo 2–9. First no-mark variations practice sample, finished with binding

Photo 2–10. Second no-mark variations practice sample, finished with binding

Thread the machine with your choice of thread. I used a variety of threads on my practice pieces. Try cotton thread in top and bobbin in a matching color. Also try some decorative threads. With these threads, I use 50/3-ply cotton thread for the bobbin in a similar color to the top thread. The type of quilting, such as background or something more visible, determines thread choice. The machine setup is the same as for free-motion quilting, page 29.

Refer to the Trace and Practice section, pages 38–52, and practice the no-mark variations in different quadrants of the samples.

Straight Lines and Variations Practice Sample

Prepare a 16" square package of two pieces of muslin and one piece of cotton batting. Mark a 1" grid on the muslin, leaving a 1" border around the edge. Mark the centermost line in each direction heavily or with a different-colored pencil to form four quadrants. Safety pin baste to hold the layers together (photo 2–11).

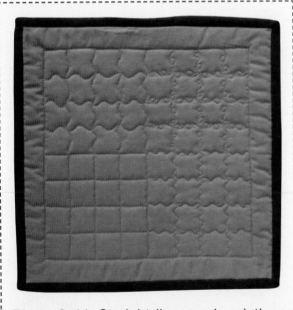

Photo 2–11. Straight lines and variations practice sample, finished with binding

Thread the machine with invisible thread on the top and 50/3-ply cotton thread in a matching color in the bobbin, or 50/3-ply cotton thread on the top and bobbin in a matching color. The machine setup is the same as for free-motion quilting, page 29.

It is helpful to know that you can free-motion quilt straight lines. It can be challenging because it is hard to stay perfectly straight and have smooth, even stitches while free-motion quilting. Try to free-motion quilt the straight lines in one of the quadrants. Start at the top of the design and work down. After a few attempts, these straight lines will get easier. It is almost impossible to have perfectly straight lines. I do this method only with invisible or closely matching thread. If using a contrasting thread, you will see some variation along the straight lines. I am more inclined to do straight lines free-motion if they are short, because it is easier to control these distances.

For crosshatching and diagonals, straight lines are a great traditional approach to quilting. Straight-line machine quilting, as discussed earlier, requires the use of the walking foot and feed dogs. With free-motion, I have more fun and am not directionally challenged. However, trying to sew straight lines free-motion results in occasional wobbles. I decided to take advantage of the wobbles by marking straight lines in a grid on the quilt, then sewing wavy lines using the straight lines as guides. Refer to the Trace and Practice section, pages 50–52, and practice crosshatch quilting on the sample.

I hope you have enjoyed these ideas. Remember the basic concepts discussed at the beginning of free-motion quilting when practicing. These things should become second nature soon.

There are 15 different trace and practice design ideas (pages 38–52). These are meant as no-mark designs. It might be helpful to trace these designs on paper first to understand each idea. Next, practice free-motion quilting each design on your practice samples. There is no need to trace on your fabric unless absolutely needed.

SECTION 2 – – – – trace and practice

Medium Stipple Practice

Starting in the upper right quadrant, evenly distribute the stitching in medium-sized puzzle-piece shapes. Work from the top left to the bottom right of the quadrant, which is how you should work on an actual quilt. If you have trouble with the shapes, trace over the diagram on paper, then try drawing on the paper yourself. You can think of the shapes as little light bulbs if puzzle pieces do not make sense. Try again to free-form stitch the shapes on the quilt package. You can trace directly on the muslin from the diagram, then sew following the lines to get started. In the long run, however, it is easier to do it free-form. Keep the stipple quilting random. The puzzle pieces should not be in rows or a pattern, but should intertwine to fill the space.

Designs were enlarged for practice and do not represent traditional stipple quilting.

Large Stipple Practice

In the second quadrant, make the puzzle shapes bigger and fill in the area evenly. It is important that you make the shapes, not the stitches, bigger. Keep the stitch length consistent throughout the quilt. This is a good practice sample for experimenting with different weights of threads to see the difference they make on the quilt.

Designs were enlarged for practice and do not represent traditional stipple quilting.

Small Stipple Practice

In the third quadrant, try small stipple quilting with a lighter-weight thread. The stitches will be less visible. I used 70-weight heirloom thread on the sample quadrant, which blends in completely. I have used 50/2-ply thread for traditional stipple quilting. This finer or lightweight thread works well when stitching heavily. Remember to keep the stitch length consistent – don't make the stitches smaller when making smaller shapes. As the traditional stipple quilting gets smaller, the longer it takes to do. On this sample, it took me at least twice as long to do the small area as compared to the medium one. Make sure you want to do this because once you start, you can't change your mind!

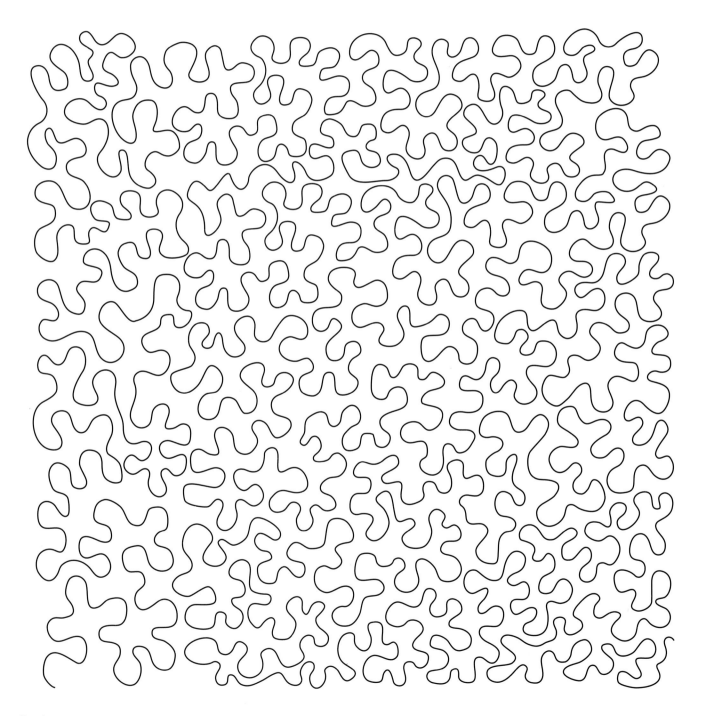

Designs were enlarged for practice and do not represent traditional stipple quilting.

Stipple Practice around a Motif

In the fourth quadrant, draw a small shape in the center of the square and free-motion stitch around it. Try traditional stipple quilting around the shape in a consistent size, starting at the top and working your way around the shape. Notice how the shape stands out once the area has been sewn. I always free-motion stitch the design first, then stipple quilt around it. This is called background quilting and the threads should blend in as much as possible.

Designs were enlarged for practice and do not represent traditional stipple quilting.

Loopy Meandering

This is a popular free-motion variation. Think of the shapes as a lowercase, cursive e and o. Make each of these letters, then continue around the quadrant. Try to fill in the area evenly, but not necessarily making each letter the same size. Sometimes it is easier to think of the loop as being made with the crossing of the threads on the top and then on the bottom. Reverse the point where the lines cross to achieve a random look. Otherwise, the stitches will be made in a row. This variation looks nice with variegated and decorative threads.

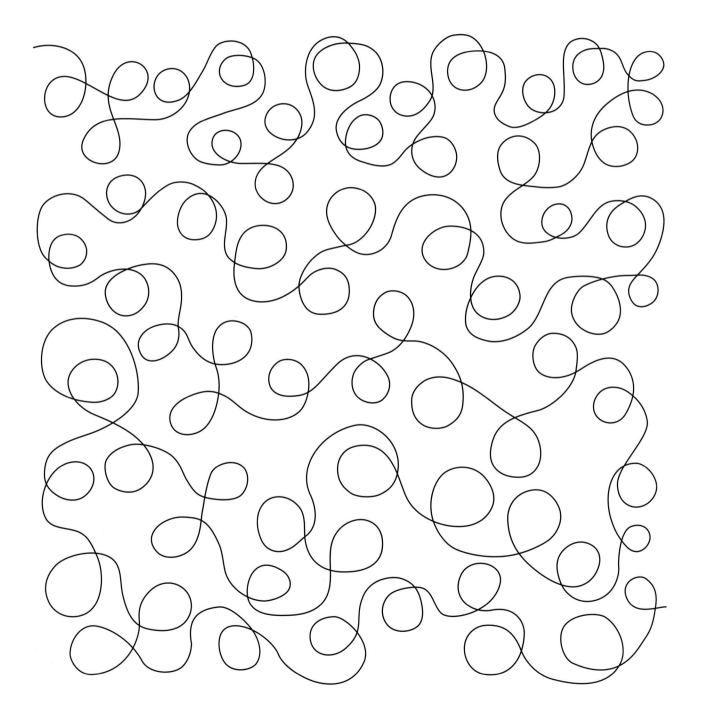

Angles and Points

This is similar to loopy meandering, except triangles are made instead of loops. This is a hard concept because most quilters are used to keeping everything circular. Sew a little slower when doing this because the stitching direction is being reversed and the threads can jam when sewing too fast. Angles and points look nice on a contemporary quilt or a quilt for a man.

Floral Stippling

Also called motif stippling, this is fun to do and any shape or design can be used. In this sample, daisies are sewn randomly in the quadrant. Sew the center circle, make petals around the circle, then sew the next circle and petals, and so on. You could use this idea for stars, hearts, leaves, and many other motifs. Your quilt's design can give you motif ideas.

Psychedelic Stippling

This is my favorite variation and I have used it on many quilts. Wanting to do something a little different in the background area on one of my quilts, I tried this spiral shape. I added a wavy line around it, moved to the next one, and so on. Make sure you stitch the spiral big enough to come back out easily and then add the wavy line. I sometimes add little spirals around the bigger spiral shapes. Use matching colored thread to make it a background design or use decorative thread for a fun, more visible look. It is called psychedelic stippling because I thought it had a 1960s feel.

Starburst

This is a similar concept to motif or floral stippling, except for the use of a starburst instead of a flower. I like this a little better than a traditional five-point star because it is easier to get around the surface area. Start at the center of the starburst and make straight lines in and out for this design. This looks great with decorative thread.

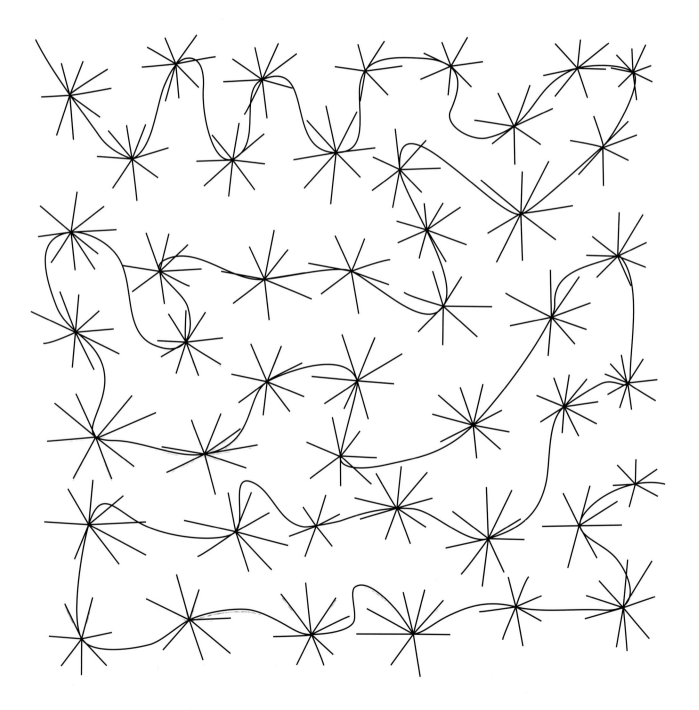

Shells

This a fun design to do. Start with a little teardrop, repeat the shape a little bigger, then a little bigger. Make another set of teardrops next to the first one. Make the next one start where the other two touched. They just keep building and billowing almost like clouds. Make either three or four teardrops in each shell, depending on the area to be filled. This is a favorite variation of my students.

SECTION 2 – – – – trace and practice

Pebbles

This fun surface design looks like a stone path or underwater bubbles. To do this, make a small circle, then another small circle next to it, and so on. To get to the next circle, you may need to resew around the circle, which creates a heavier line of thread. The look is a thicker, almost surface embellishment.

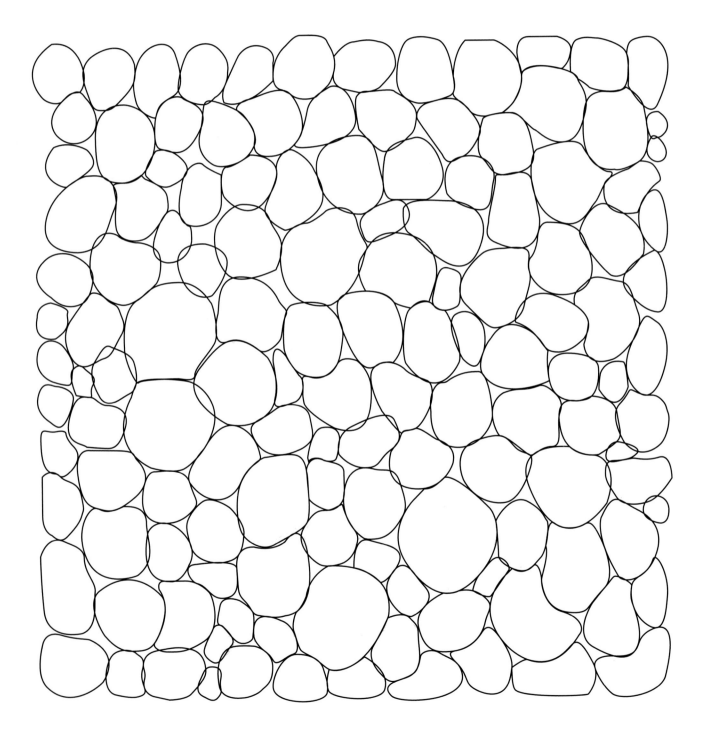

Echo Quilting

This stitching echoes a shape, appliqué design, pieced area, or quilting design. True echo quilting resembles the concentric circles that get bigger when a pebble is dropped in a pond. For this reason, it is not always best for free-motion because you have to stop and start often. I echo quilt mainly with one or two lines to outline a shape or design, using the darning foot as a guide. My darning foot is a circle and it rests about ¼" from the shape I am outlining. Try this idea by echoing around a shape such as a heart.

Curvy Crosshatching

Curvy crosshatching looks great and is fast and easy. Try these wavy lines on one of the marked quadrants in your sample. Don't worry about the waves being the same from row to row. I like it better when they don't match, producing great little shapes throughout the quilt. However, they should be similar in scale.

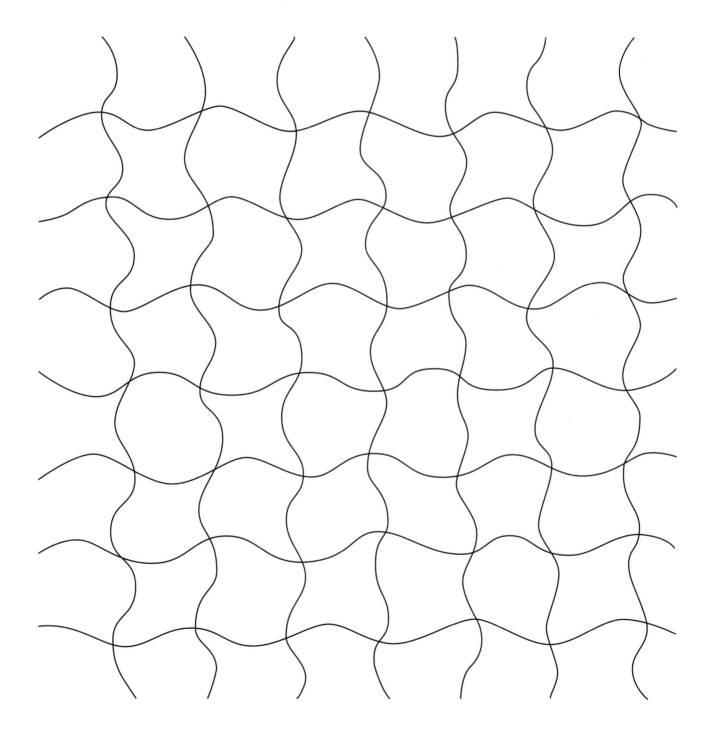

Small Curvy Crosshatching

In the next quadrant of the sample, vary the scale of the wavy line for a different look from curvy crosshatching.

Loopy Crosshatching

Take Curvy Crosshatching one step further and sew loopy shapes along the straight lines in the next quadrant of the sample. Sew an e and o, then cross an intersection and sew them again, and so on. Two loops crossing at the intersection create a sloppy look.

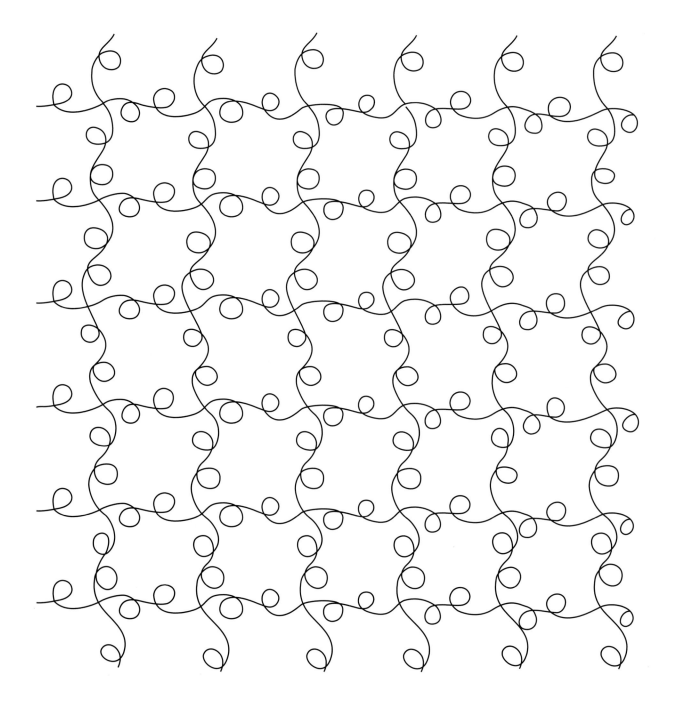

Marked Designs

Cables and other motif-type designs help fill a specific area with stitching. For the type of traditional quilts I make, it is important to be able to use these designs. They must be marked on the quilt top before it is basted, which is discussed more thoroughly in Section Three. Some quilters do not enjoy these designs because of the time they take to mark. Hopefully, with good instruction and tools that make it easier, this step will be more enjoyable. Because feathers, cables, and other types of traditional designs are my favorites, I am willing to take the time to mark them to achieve the desired result

(photo 2–12). Following lines that have been marked on the top takes control when free-motion quilting. This is why no-mark designs are so popular. With practice, it becomes easier to follow the lines. Here are some helpful suggestions.

Think of the marked lines as guidelines. Try to stay as close to them as possible, but if you stray, gradually and smoothly come closer to the line again. A quick jerk back to the line is very noticeable. As long as you stay true to the design, it will look like the design you wanted once the marking is gone. This does not mean you are lowering your standards for free-motion quilting, it is just a different standard to

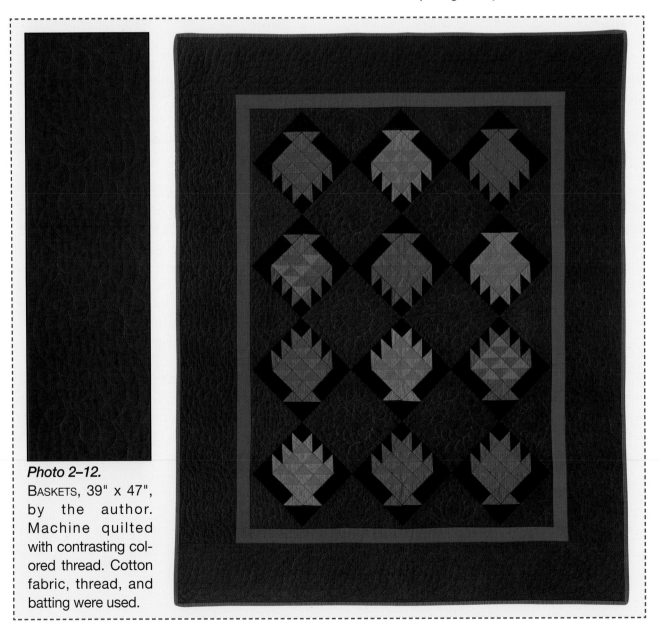

Photo 2–12.
BASKETS, 39" x 47", by the author. Machine quilted with contrasting colored thread. Cotton fabric, thread, and batting were used.

help you relax. It is hard to stay perfectly on the line at all times. I stay close to my lines because of many hours of practice, but I am not always perfectly on the line.

Start at the top of the design and work down. This way, you can always see the line that you need to follow. Sometimes, you may want to sew backward to save time. Some quilters can do this without much trouble, while others have a harder time because the darning foot gets in the way visually. I rarely sew backward because my stitches are never as smooth and consistent. Try both ways for yourself and see what you think.

A frequently asked question is where should you look when free-motion quilting. A good comparison is to think of driving a car. When driving, your hands are on the steering wheel, but you are watching the road ahead. The steering wheel is visible, but you need to have sight of the road ahead. In free-motion quilting, you need to see where you are going, but also be aware of the needle.

Continuous-line designs offer the advantage of few starting and stopping stitches. Sometimes, a design can be made continuous by changing the way you quilt it. You can break the design into two paths and make it more continuous, as with the sample heart design, page 55. You can also make a design continuous by resewing a small area, as with the sample feather design, page 59.

Practice Sample

Prepare a 10" square package of two pieces of muslin and one piece of batting. Mark the designs provided on one piece of muslin by laying the

muslin on top of the patterns (page 55) and tracing with a silver marking pencil. Safety pin baste to hold layers together (photo 2–13).

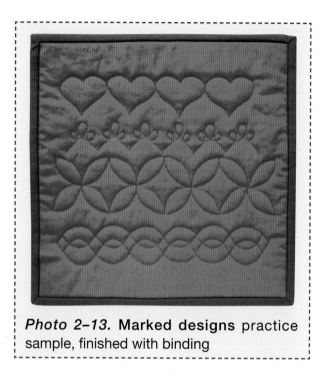

Photo 2–13. **Marked designs** practice sample, finished with binding

Thread the machine with invisible thread on the top and matching cotton thread in the bobbin, or matching cotton thread in the top and bobbin. If you are a beginner, it is a good idea to use thread that blends with your fabric because it takes more control to follow the lines. The machine setup is the same as for free-motion quilting, page 29. Continuous-line designs are the easiest marked designs to sew.

The loop design on the sample consists of one continuous line, which will be sewn in one path (fig. 2–11). Just follow the design as it is drawn, sewing the little loop, big loop, and little loop.

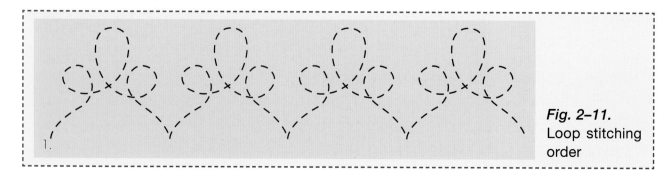

Fig. 2–11. Loop stitching order

Practice Sample Designs

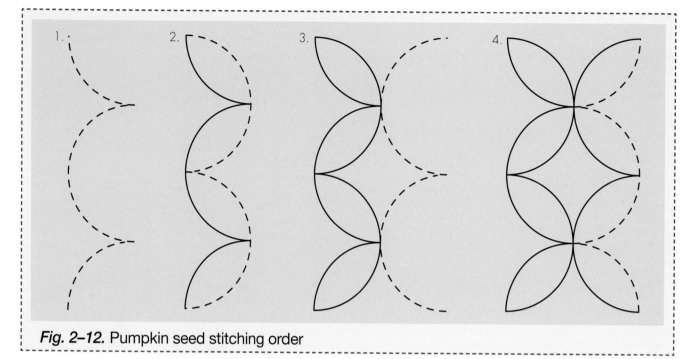

Fig. 2–12. Pumpkin seed stitching order

Repeat down the line. Remember to start at the top of the pattern and work down so you can see the line in front of you as you sew. Position the practice sample so the bulk is always to the left. Sew this first marked design and see how it looks. Sometimes it is better to look at the back of the quilt once you have sewn to see the design without the marked lines.

The pumpkin seed design is continuous, even though it may not look that way. Start at the top and sew half circles down the design. Go back to the top and sew another row of half circles. This design takes four paths (fig. 2–12). This design is easy to do and can be marked over the surface of an entire quilt, making a great allover pattern.

The heart design is another pattern that does not appear to be continuous. Think of it as breaking the pattern in half and sewing the bottom of the hearts. Stop and come back to the top of the quilt to sew the top of the hearts (fig. 2–13). Using two paths, this becomes a great continuous-line design.

The cable design is a simple pattern that requires four paths (fig. 2–14, page 57). Start sewing at the top of the design for more control. After the first path, you could try sewing back-

ward from the bottom of the cable. Occasionally, there is a student who does well sewing backward with no trouble seeing the lines. Remember to treat the practice sample as an actual quilt, and to start the next path from the top of the quilt. Turning the quilt once you reach the bottom of the path places the bulk under the arm of the machine, making it much harder to handle.

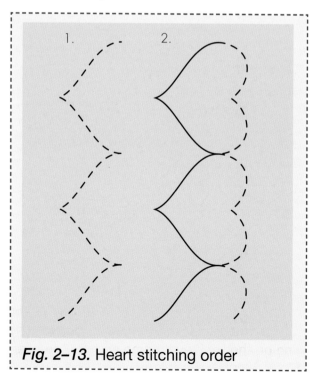

Fig. 2–13. Heart stitching order

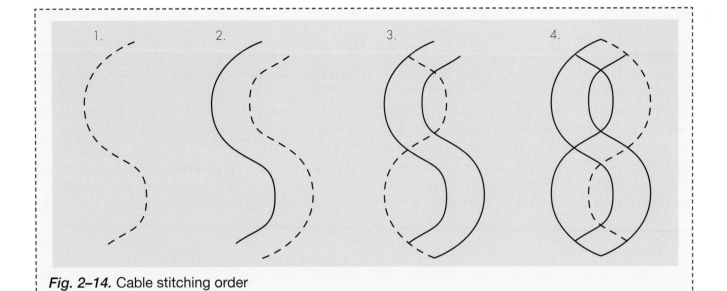

Fig. 2–14. Cable stitching order

Helpful Hints

Try to reposition your hands at an inconspicuous area in the design, such as a point or intersection (photo 2–14). When starting again, the first stitch won't be in a noticeable place. If you reposition your hands in the middle of a long, curved line it can be more noticeable.

The question of how to take stitching out, or what to do if bobbin thread runs out, often arises. I take stitching out all the time. Just take the stitches back out to an inconspicuous area, then start the new stitching a few stitches into the previous ones, making small securing stitches over these. Be careful not to take stitching out too often. If you become overly focused on a specific area and think that every stitch should be removed, that's all you will be doing. Instead, place a safety pin in the questionable areas, go back after the quilt is finished, and decide what really needs to be redone.

Don't get discouraged at this point. As a beginner, following marked designs is hard to do and it takes practice. It also takes a little determination, so hang in there.

Fig. 2–14. Repositioning the quilt

Feathers

I would rather free-motion quilt a feather than any other design. Feathers are forgiving and look nice when they aren't exactly perfect. Not sewing on the lines every time adds to the beauty of this natural, organic design. A nice rhythm is developed when sewing a feather. The two types of feathers presented, open and traditional, are each approached a little differently (photo 2–15, page 58). I hope you enjoy these wonderful designs as much as I do.

Practice Samples

Prepare two 10" square packages of two pieces of muslin and one piece of cotton batting for each. For the first package, mark the open and traditional feathers by laying one piece of muslin over the patterns (page 59) and tracing with a silver marking pencil. For the second package, mark the plume feather and curved line (page 60) in the same way. Safety pin baste to hold the layers together (photos 2–16 and 2–17, page 61).

Thread the machine with invisible thread on the top and matching 50/3-ply cotton thread in the bobbin, or matching 50/3-ply cotton thread in the top and bobbin. The machine setup is the same as for free-motion quilting, page 29.

To free-motion quilt the feather design, it is important to understand how the feather is made. Most feathers have a center spine with

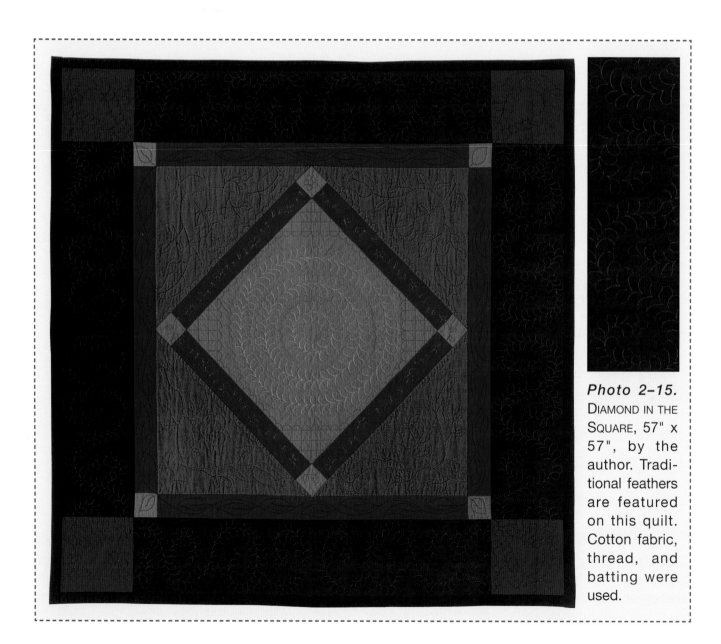

Photo 2–15. Diamond in the Square, 57" x 57", by the author. Traditional feathers are featured on this quilt. Cotton fabric, thread, and batting were used.

Open and Traditional Feathers

Plume Feather and Spine for Free-Form Feather

Photo 2-16. Feather practice sample, finished with binding

Photo 2-17. Feather practice sample, finished with binding

feathers on one or both sides of the spine. There are many variations such as feather wreaths, feather hearts, etc.

The traditional feather takes three paths to sew. In relationship to the top of the quilt, start at the top of the feather (Feather Direction, page 62). Sew the center spine first. If the feather is on a border, sew the center spine down the entire border. Come back to the top of the feather and sew one side of the feather. Sew the teardrop-shaped feather to the center spine, then resew to get to the next feather. Continue in this manner until one side of the feather is complete. Come back to the top and sew the other side of the feather to complete the design (fig. 2-15).

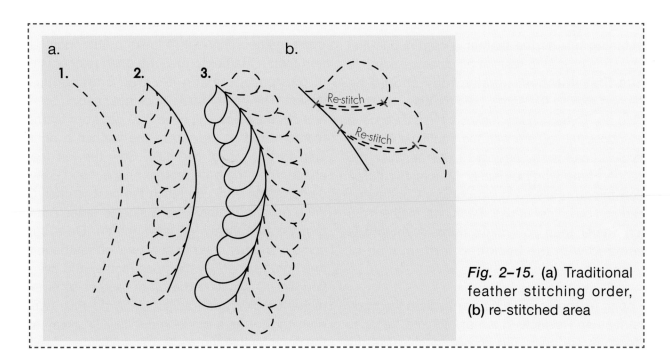

Fig. 2-15. (a) Traditional feather stitching order, (b) re-stitched area

Feather Direction

A frequently asked question is whether there is a top or bottom to the feather design. This can be confusing. I suggest you sew from the top of the feather down, which means the top in relationship to the quilt itself. The feather can be drawn with the round part of the teardrop shape down or up. Some people think one direction might be easier to sew than the other. The main consideration is how the design is positioned on the quilt (fig. 2–16). Also, some quilters think one side of the feather design is easier than the other. When beginning, I thought the left side was a little easier than the right. Teach yourself to be comfortable with either side. Now, I am completely feather ambidextrous.

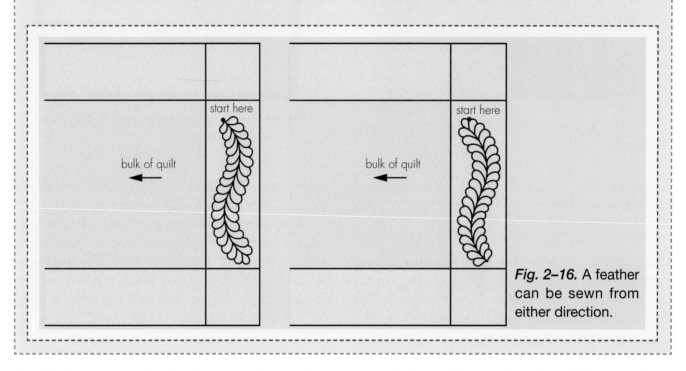

start here

bulk of quilt

start here

bulk of quilt

Fig. 2–16. A feather can be sewn from either direction.

Restitching makes the feather a continuous-line design. It is crucial to restitch as close as possible to the first stitches. Ideally, they should be restitched exactly the same, hole for hole, which is hard to do. Thread choice makes a big difference in how successful you are with the traditional feather. Invisible thread is the easiest to use because the restitched area won't be seen. Matching colored cotton thread is also a good choice. Contrasting thread can be harder to use. Traditional feathers are much easier than you might think. A rhythm is developed with the back and forth motion of sewing.

The open feather is sewn differently than the traditional feather. Restitching is not required because the feathers are open and do not touch. I like the open feather, although it looks a little more like a fern than a feather to me. The open feather is done in one path, making it a true continuous-line design. The center spine does not need to be sewn first because you will need it to get from feather to feather. Start at the top of the feather in relationship to the top of the quilt. Sew the left feather shape, then the right feather shape. Next, sew the center spine until you reach the next feather. Continue sewing feathers from side to side. The pattern will not always go left-right-left. On a curved spine, you may need to sew two left feathers, then one right feather. Try the open feather and see how you like it. I outline the open feather at times to make it look more traditional. To do this, use the darning foot as a guide and follow ¼" away along the open feather (fig. 2–17, page 63).

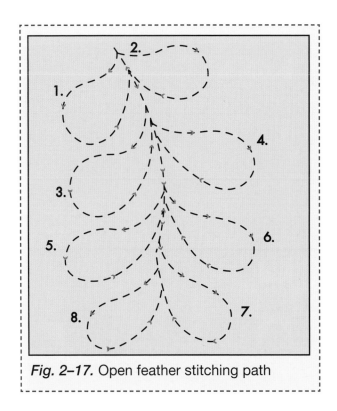

Fig. 2–17. Open feather stitching path

The plume feather has more elongated feathers. The stitching order may be different on these feathers, otherwise, the restitched area would be long. With this alternate method, the restitching is done in shorter areas. Starting at the top, sew the center spine first. Come back to the top and sew the first feather, then re-stitch along the center spine to get to the next feather. Sew this feather completely until it touches the previous feather on the outside. Restitch this outer portion to get to the next feather (fig. 2–18). Contin-

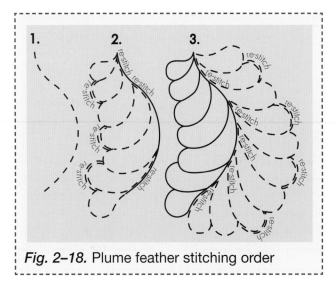

Fig. 2–18. Plume feather stitching order

ue in this manner to complete the feathers on one side. Come back to the top and sew the other side of the feather. Restitching every other feather at the spine and the outside curved area works well for these long plume designs.

The free-form feather is another variation. Once you are comfortable with the open feather and are proficient at sewing the feather shape, try this free-form style. Draw a simple curved line for the center spine and sew. Then, free-form stitch the feather shape on either side of the spine (fig. 2–19). You could switch to a decorative thread to see how you like a contrasting thread. These feathers do not always look consistent in size, but are really fun and can free you from having to mark the complete feather on the quilt top. This can be a great overall design. Just draw the center spine

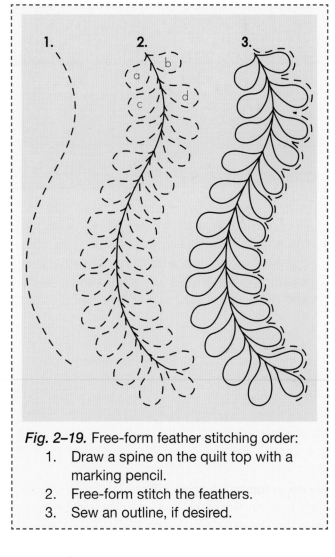

Fig. 2–19. Free-form feather stitching order:
1. Draw a spine on the quilt top with a marking pencil.
2. Free-form stitch the feathers.
3. Sew an outline, if desired.

Photo 2–18. ASHLEY'S STARS, 44½" x 56", by the author. This free-form star quilt was easily free-motion quilted with curvy crosshatching and free-form feathers. Cotton fabric, cotton and metallic threads, and cotton-blend batting were used.

spaced evenly across the quilt, then free-form stitch the open feathers. One of my favorite quilts is ASHLEY'S STARS (photo 2–18, page 64), which was quilted with curvy crosshatching and free-form feathers with metallic thread in the border. It was a quick and easy way to quilt.

You may want to practice some of the feathers in the last section of book that are used in the projects. Make some more 10" practice samples with these feathers marked on them. There are two variations on the feathered wreath, a feathered heart, a motif-style feather, and a few border feathers. These are all traditional feathers and good practice designs. Sometimes when sewing a feathered wreath, you will find you are sewing half of the wreath backward. You can split the wreath in half and work from the top down. This is how I sew the feathered heart. The stitching order is presented with these designs.

You have now completed almost 10 practice samples to learn the techniques and should be feeling more comfortable with machine quilting. Straight-line machine quilting with the walking foot is the easiest technique and free-motion quilting is more challenging. Most students enjoy free-motion quilting after some practice; however, it can be frustrating at first. I have tried to come up with words of encouragement for my students over the years. They sometimes feel discouraged, especially after the exercises with marked designs and feathers. This is my pep talk for anyone who feels frustrated.

It is easy to say that to become a good free-motion quilter you need to practice, practice, practice. It takes about 100 hours of practice to feel really comfortable with free-motion skills. However, I think you need more encouraging words than just to practice more. Quilters tend to want everything perfect the first time they try a technique. It is not going happen with free-motion quilting. To become good, you have to be determined and a little stubborn. I definitely got mad at first and was not going let it get the best of me. I was determined to practice and conquer this technique.

This is a different skill compared to anything else you have ever done. Free-motion quilting is often compared to drawing. This can be a little intimidating because it implies you have to be an artist to free-motion quilt. I don't feel this is true. There have been artists in my classes who have the exact same learning curve with free-motion skills as anyone else in class. If you are artistic, you may be able to come up with creative ways to quilt or creative uses of thread, but the skills of free-motion stitching are learned the same way.

Free-motion quilting is better compared to cursive handwriting. This was a skill learned in grade school that took many hours of practice for proficiency. We practiced making the letters over and over on lined paper until comfortable with them. With handwriting, the pencil moves while the paper stays in the same spot. It is opposite with free-motion quilting. The pencil, or needle, is stationary and the paper, or quilt, is moving. It is awkward at first, but becomes easier with practice. It takes repetition to become comfortable, just like when you learned cursive handwriting. Another challenge is moving an object that could be as large as 80" x 100" – your quilt. This is discussed further in the next section. I hope my pep talk has helped and that you will be a little easier on yourself because you are doing great (photo 2–19, page 66).

Photo 2–19. BLUE TULIPS ON PINK SKIES, 76" x 81", by the author. Machine quilted in a traditional style with feathers, stipple quilting, and curvy lines. Quilting designs were inspired by Amish Bars quilts. Cotton fabric, threads, and cotton-blend batting were used.

Every student who takes a machine-quilting class wants to eventually be able to quilt a quilt, not just work on practice samples. Part of the learning process is how to achieve smooth, even stitches while handling the bulk of the quilt. I recommend practicing on the small samples, but it is also important to work on quilts. This is a part of the learning process. Some practice projects are provided in Section Four. After reading this section, try one or more of these projects and treat them as practice quilts. These small projects are a stepping stone to your next real quilt project. They are a great way to learn and will give you the confidence you need on your quilts.

Choosing Quilting Designs

"Quilt as desired" is a common phrase in piecing and appliqué books. This leaves the beginner confused and frustrated, mainly because there is nowhere to turn for advice on this subject. There are many factors that go into deciding how to quilt a quilt.

Let your top tell you how it should be quilted. If it is heavily pieced, the quilting will play a supporting role (photos 3–1, below, and 3–2, page 68). If there

Photo 3–1. ALYSSA'S PINK PIN-WHEELS, 71" x 80", by Pat Holly, Muskegon, Michigan. In this heavily pieced quilt, the quilting takes on a supporting role. Cotton fabric and batting, and nylon and cotton thread were used.

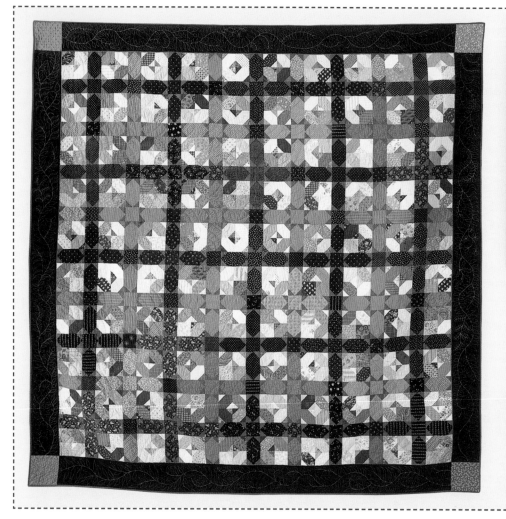

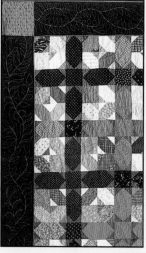

Photo 3–2. A Simple Quilt, Really, 93" x 93", by Pat Holly. This quilt contains a beautifully free-motion quilted flower and leaf border, and a simple approach to the pieced center. Cotton fabric and batting, and nylon and cotton thread were used.

are several open areas for fancy designs, the quilting will play a major role. On heavily pieced tops, it is best to use an allover-type of design, such as pumpkin seed, shells, straight-line crosshatching, or curvy crosshatching.

The style of the quilt can help you determine the style of quilting. If it is Amish style, feathers and cables are popular choices. If it is a nineteenth-century style, you could use designs from that era, such as floral motifs, feathers, stippling, and crosshatching (photo 3–3, page 69). If it is modern, consider some fun and funky ideas, such as the variations on stipple quilting from Section Two.

Determining if the quilt is formal or informal helps you decide whether you want an informal free-form, no-mark type of design (photo 3–4,

page 69) or a more structured, formal design that fits evenly within the space it is filling. Another important consideration is how much you like to quilt. If you love it like me, you will choose to quilt more heavily and take more time. If this is your least favorite part, you may want to choose a quick and easy approach. Either way is fine, as long as you quilt within the guidelines of your batting.

The method used to quilt makes a difference in deciding how to quilt. A machine quilter's choices are different than those of a hand quilter. One of the differences is the type of design. In hand quilting, you have the ability to travel underneath the surface from place to place. In machine quilting, the designs should be as continuous as

Photo 3–3. LE PANIER DE FLEURS, 67" x 78", by the author. This award-winning quilt was machine quilted in a traditional and formal style, with feathers, stipple quilting, and free-motion straight lines in the crosshatching. Cotton fabric, thread, and cotton-blend batting were used.

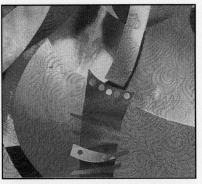

Photo 3–4. THREE AMIGOS, 51" x 46", by Melody Johnson, Cary, Illinois. This is a wonderful example of free-form, no-mark machine quilting in an informal style. Constructed from hand-dyed cotton and silk fabrics, this quilt was fused directly to the cotton batting.

possible because you have to stop and start again to move from place to place (fig. 3–1). It is best to minimize these stops and starts as much as possible.

Fig. 3–1. A continuous-line design is the best choice for machine quilting.

Another difference from hand quilting is handling the bulk at the sewing machine. Placing more complex designs in easy-to-handle places on the quilt is helpful to the beginner. For example, place complex designs in the borders and simple designs in the center area (fig. 3–2). After reading about handling bulk, page 79, you will have a better understanding of how this makes a

Fig. 3–2. The strategic placement of designs makes quilting easier.

difference in choosing designs (photo 3–5, page 71). The method of sewing can also make quilting easier in particular areas. For instance, it may be easier to free-motion stitch straight lines on a pieced block, rather than sewing them with a walking foot (fig. 3–3, page 71).

It is important to make sure your quilt is quilted evenly. With the machine, it is easy to heavily sew one area and lightly sew another. This makes the quilt lie unevenly and look unattractive. If you heavily sew an area, with feathers and stipple quilting for instance, the other areas need be sewn with the same density. You can use something that gives the surface the same amount of quilting, possibly crosshatching. As long as you follow the guidelines for your batting, a quilt can look nice with a minimum amount of quilting if it is evenly and appropriately sewn. Also make sure the designs fill the area completely. A 5" feather design is not large enough for a 10" block. These Amish quilts have

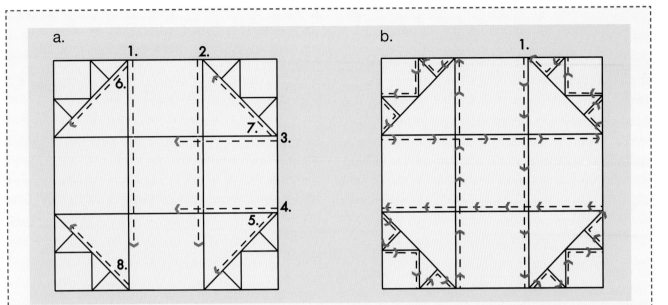

Fig. 3–3. (a) Straight stitching with a walking foot on this block requires repackaging the quilt four times and numerous starts and stops. (b) Free-motion quilting this block requires no repackaging and one start and stop.

Photo 3–5. Turkey Tears, 83½" x 100½", by the author. The blocks were pieced by the 2nd Friday Quilters. A big quilt can be quilted on the home sewing machine with well-balanced placement of quilting designs. Cotton fabric, thread, and cotton-blend batting were used.

well-proportioned designs, without being heavily quilted (photos 3–6, below, and 3–7, page 73).

My approach to choosing quilting designs might be a little different than most. When I was a hand quilter, I enjoyed figuring out how to quilt the top. For me, quilting is as important as any other part. I love to design the top and choose fabrics, but also love planning the quilting designs and quilting. While designing my quilt, I think about how to quilt it and rarely have a top completed without knowing how it will be quilted. This affects the style, as well as the fabric choices.

For areas that will have beautiful quilting designs, choose solid or solid-like fabrics so the designs will be visible. On a busy print, the designs won't show unless you use a highly decorative thread

(photo 3–8, page 74). While piecing and appliquéing a top, I constantly re-evaluate my choices for quilting, thinking about how they will look and whether they will be manageable during the quilting process. Make quilting a priority and part of the entire plan.

Study quilts to get ideas for designs. I look at antique quilt books for ideas on the placement of the designs. Use of a magnifying glass helps to better see the designs. These old quilts can generate wonderful and unique ideas. I am also inspired at quilt shows, where I mainly focus on quilting designs and search for original ideas

A great way to see how your chosen designs will fit on the quilt top is to use inexpensive tracing paper (see page 22). Draw the designs on the

Photo 3–6. BARS, 57" x 57", by Pat Holly. Cotton fabric, thread, and batting were used.

Photo 3–7. NINE-PATCH, 43" x 51", by Pat Holly. Machine quilted with contrasting-colored cotton threads. Cotton fabric, thread, and batting were used.

Photo 3–8. FOLK GARDEN APPLIQUÉ SAMPLER, 63½" x 75", by the author. The border was machine quilted with a bright poly-neon thread for the designs to show on the print fabric. Cotton fabric, cotton and polyester thread, and cotton-blend batting were used.

paper and lay it on the quilt to see if you like the look and if it fills the area completely. Sometimes tracing with your finger over the quilt top can help you visualize the designs, but using the tracing paper is better because you can see the quilting take shape. Many times I have changed my mind about a design after doing this.

The quilt should be quilted the way you want, according to your likes and needs. I am always thinking of how to make my job as a machine quilter easier and how to handle bulk at the sewing machine. Make sure designs fill the areas nicely and the entire surface is quilted evenly (photo 3–9).

Marking

Now that you have determined your quilting pattern, it is time to mark the top. For some quilters, marking the top is their least favorite step in the quiltmaking process. For traditional-type designs such as feathers and cables, it is necessary to mark the top. There are ways to make this step easier and less intimidating. Finding the right tools is an important step. Marking tools should be easy to use and come off the fabric easily when ready. A good quality fabric marking pencil takes the chore out of this step.

Photo 3–9. NEW YORK STATE OF MIND, 69" x 69", by Pat Holly and the author. This quilt was heavily machine quilted with traditional feathers and stippling. Cotton fabric, thread, and cotton-blend batting were used.

Press the quilt top before marking because most marking tools are adversely affected by heat. Begin by marking any straight lines on your top. If you are stitching in the ditch, you don't need to mark those lines because you will follow the seam line. Diagonals or crosshatching need to be marked. Use quilters' rulers for marking straight lines. They have 45-degree markings and help keep your straight lines and diagonals accurately aligned. Some machines have guides to use with the walking foot for sewing straight lines at even intervals; however, marking the actual lines provides the most accuracy.

If you use patterns from a book, the easiest way to mark them is to make a copy of the pattern, place it under the fabric, and trace the design. You might need to tape the design to the table as well as the quilt so it doesn't shift. Patterns from books can be enlarged or reduced to make them fit the area perfectly. Tracing a pattern works well for light-colored fabrics. If the fabric is dark and you can't see the design to mark, you need to use a light box (see page 22). Tape the pattern on the light box, then lay the quilt top over the pattern, and trace the design. This works even when marking on black fabric. When using a light box, be careful not to mark heavily with the pencil. You may press too hard and get a dark line that is difficult to remove.

The use of purchased stencils is an easy option for marking. Just lay the stencil on top of the fabric and mark through the cut-out lines on the stencil. Your pencil needs to be sharp to fit along these lines. The size of the design cannot be altered with a stencil, so you should find one that fits the area you need. However, there are ways to make minor adjustments. A stencil shape can be made larger by adding a row of outline stitching to the design. I have used border stencils successfully by starting in the middle of the border and working toward the corners. If the stencil is slightly shorter than needed, add a little extra from the stencil shape to make it fit. Do this first on tracing paper to know exactly how to adjust the size. With a little planning, you can make a stencil usable, even if it is not the perfect size for the area.

With lightweight cardboard or template plastic, you can make your own stencils, which is a good solution for many marking situations. Simply transfer the design to cardboard with carbon paper or glue the design to the cardboard. Cut out the shape with scissors or a sharp blade. Cut slots for the inside lines of the design with a sharp blade, leaving connecting plastic so the template does not fall apart. If you use template plastic, lay the plastic over the quilt design and trace. Cut out the shape with scissors or a sharp blade. For inside lines, cut thin slots. I use hand-made stencils frequently for simple shapes such as circle, pumpkin seed, clamshell, and fan designs.

Designing your own quilting patterns can make marking easier and more personal. There are many wonderful books, workshops, and conferences that teach these skills. If you don't enjoy the step of marking the top, it is best to choose no-mark designs. Marking my quilt has allowed me to have beautiful designs that I love.

Backing Fabric

Choosing appropriate backing fabric makes your job easier. I like to use a small, busy print that coordinates with the quilt top. This allows me to use thread in the bobbin that is a similar color to the thread used on the top of the quilt. If the color of the backing fabric contrasts with the colors in the top, the use of highly contrasting threads in the top and bobbin will cause tension-related discrepancies. There will always be either a little of the bobbin thread showing on the top or a little top thread showing on the back. The tensions need to be as perfect as possible, but it is nearly impossible not to see little dots of thread when you have high contrast between the top and bobbin thread color. A busy print allows the bobbin thread to blend nicely and hides some of the imperfections of machine quilting that can show on the back. You can easily change the thread color in the bobbin to coordinate with the thread on the top. I like to showcase the beautiful machine stitching on the front of the quilt and prefer the back to have a more blended and subtle look (photo 3–10).

Diamond in the Square backing, page 58

Feather Sampler backing, page 97

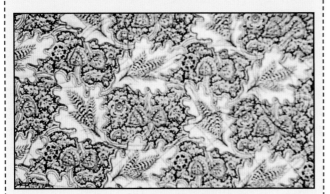

Le Panier de Fleurs backing, page 69

Photo 3–10.
Coordinating prints for backing fabric

Le Panier de Fleurs has both dark and light fabric on the top, so I chose a busy navy and tan print for the back. When quilting with tan thread on the top, I used tan thread in the bobbin, and when

quilting with navy thread on the top, I used navy thread in the bobbin. There are many quilters who love to do back art and use decorative or contrasting threads in the bobbin. This is another approach and can be done successfully.

Cut the backing fabric and batting about 2" larger than the quilt top on all sides. For example, if the top is 45" x 45", the backing and batting should be about 49" x 49". This extends the quilt for sewing the borders. It is hard to free-motion quilt the borders if there is nothing to hold while sewing near the outer edges. If necessary, piece the backing for large projects.

Basting

A well-basted quilt is a foundation for successful machine quilting. There are many methods available, and whichever method you choose, it is important to take the time to do a good job. I have had good results with safety pin basting and am reluctant to change a good thing. That does not mean this is the only successful way to baste. The following are some different basting methods.

Safety Pin Basting

To prepare for basting, press the backing and quilt top, unless it is marked. The top should be pressed before marking as previously mentioned because most marking tools are adversely affected by heat.

Mark the center of each side on both the backing and quilt top to help you align the quilt accurately. Lay the backing wrong side up on either a large table or the floor, depending on the size of the quilt. Tape the sides of the backing every 4"–5" with masking tape. If you baste on a carpeted floor, which I do, use T-pins to hold the backing to the carpet. Do not tightly stretch or distort the backing fabric. It should be smooth and not have any fullness. If the backing is stretched too tightly, it will be uneven with the top.

Lay the batting on the backing, smoothing any fullness or wrinkles. Some battings need to be taken out of the package for a while and unrolled to breathe and relax any creases. Next, place the marked quilt top right side up on the batting, matching the center marks so the top and backing align evenly. Smooth the top, being careful not to stretch or pull.

On larger quilts, measure at this point to see if the quilt is square and even. Measure side to side, top to bottom, and across the diagonals. If there is a difference, readjust the top and measure again. It is easy to distort large tops by aggressively smoothing. This is the reason I prefer laying out the complete backing, batting, and top versus methods that baste in sections. Refer to "Basting a Large Quilt," page 79, for an alternative method that helps with handling bulk.

Refer to page 23 for the description of safety pins. Pin the initial cross as shown in figure 3–4. Starting in the center of the quilt, place pins outward to the edge in the order shown. Leave the pins open and close them once they are all in place because the process of closing the pins can pull the backing and cause puckers. Place safety pins every 4" when using cotton batting and every 3" when using polyester and wool battings.

Some quilters like to move large quilts off the floor after pinning the initial cross (lines 1–4) because it is more comfortable for their backs and knees. If you prefer this, remove the tape or T-pins and carefully move the quilt package to a table. Continue pinning in quadrants (quadrants 5–8), carefully moving the quilt to get to the next quadrant. The quilt can be moved successfully at this point. Fill the remaining quadrants with the proper amount of pins. You don't have to avoid placing pins on or near quilting designs because they will be taken out at the sewing machine when you get close to them. It is important to have the proper amount of pins in the quilt to hold it securely.

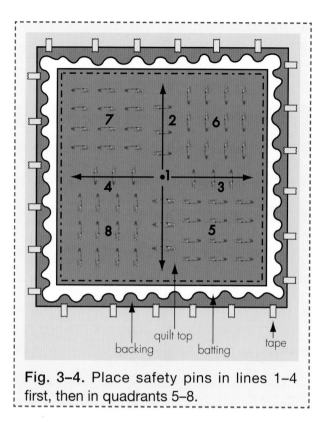

quilt top
backing   batting   tape

Fig. 3–4. Place safety pins in lines 1–4 first, then in quadrants 5–8.

If you have not done so already, you can now remove the tape or T-pins from the layers. Close all the safety pins. Tools made specifically for this purpose are invaluable because it is hard on your fingers to close all the pins (see Products, page 110). The last step in the basting process is to thread baste the outer edge of the quilt top to the batting and backing to neatly secure it during the quilting process. Thread baste by hand about ¼" from the edge of the quilt top with a large running stitch. This, combined with the extra 2" of backing and batting, extends the quilt, making it possible to free-motion stitch the borders.

Safety pin basting is time consuming, but this is one area where saving time is not the most important issue. The secret to successful machine quilting is a well-basted quilt, so however you choose to baste, do a good job. The following are some additional basting methods. For each method, follow the same first step of taping or T-pinning the backing to the table or floor and mark the center of each side of the backing and top.

Basting Gun

Very popular a few years ago, this gun allows you to insert a plastic tab through the layers of the quilt. A large needle pokes through the layers and inserts the tab. Make sure you place the tab down and up, like a safety pin. If the tab just goes down through the layers, it is not tight enough to hold the layers securely. Place the tabs in the same order as the safety pins. Remove tabs at the sewing machine by carefully clipping when close to them. Once the quilting is finished, remove any remaining tabs. To assure you won't clip the fabric, some of the guns come with a cutter. A disadvantage to the gun is that some quilters feel the large needle can make holes in the fabric. However, this method can be successful and is helpful for quilters who have a hard time opening and closing the safety pins. It takes about the same amount of time to baste with the basting gun as with safety pins.

Spray Basting Adhesive

This is a popular product for basting and there are many approaches to this method. Make sure you are in a well-ventilated area or outside when spray basting. Spray the wrong side of the backing and tape or T-pin it to the table or floor. Carefully lay the batting on the backing. Spray the wrong side of the quilt top and carefully lay it on the batting. This step is easier to do with two people when working on a larger quilt.

Spray basting works well for small projects. When working on large projects, I experienced shifting of the layers because I repackage often. It is helpful to add some safety pins after spray basting larger quilts. A concern for many quilters is the fumes these products have. Always work in a well-ventilated area or outside. Spray only the backing and top because, if the product gets on your table or floor, it is hard to remove. This method is definitely quicker than safety pin basting, but has some drawbacks.

Fusible Batting

There are many fusible battings on the market, including cotton, polyester, and cotton/polyester blends. To prepare the quilt package, tape or T-pin the backing fabric to the table or floor, then lay the fusible batting down. Lay the top over the batting. Follow the specific directions on your fusible batting for heat settings. Most of these battings require a steam iron to fuse. Steam iron in place for five seconds and continue across the entire surface. Turn the quilt over and repeat the steaming process on the back. This batting stays secure throughout the quilting process. This method takes about the same amount of time as safety pin basting. It is not recommended for use on a marked top because the steam and heat could adversely affect the markings.

Handling Bulk
Basting a Large Quilt

When quilting a queen or king-sized quilt, it is hard to handle the bulk at the sewing machine. One way to manage these bigger projects is to not include all of the batting during a portion of the quilting process. To do this, tape or T-pin the backing to the floor. Lay the batting over the backing, then place the top evenly over the batting. Mark the centers of each side of both the backing and top. Measure side to side and on the diagonals. To this point, the steps are exactly the same as safety pin basting.

Next, safety pin baste the center third of the quilt top (fig. 3–5, page 80). Carefully roll back the right side of the top and cut away the right third of the batting in a curved line (fig. 3–6, page 80). Indicating that this is the top right side, carefully roll the batting and set aside. Lay the top over the backing and gently roll the backing and top to the point where pinned. Follow the same steps for the left side of the package.

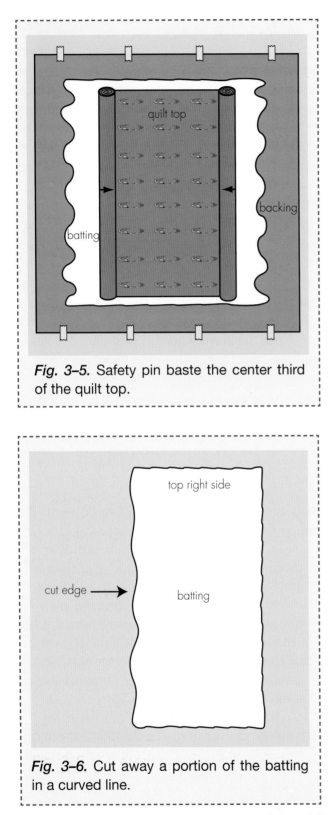

Fig. 3–5. Safety pin baste the center third of the quilt top.

Fig. 3–6. Cut away a portion of the batting in a curved line.

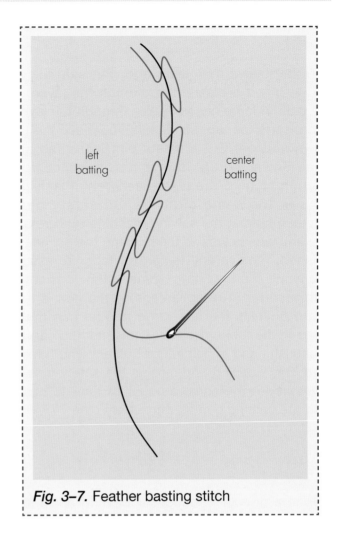

Fig. 3–7. Feather basting stitch

along the curved line. Do not overlap the battings. Use a needle and thread to weave the two pieces together with a feather basting stitch (fig. 3–7). Lay the quilt top down and baste the right side. Once this area is quilted, repeat these steps for the left side.

Stitching Order

Once the quilt is marked and basted, it is time to decide the quilting order. This is the point when I figure out my plan of attack, so to speak. The order for quilting is provided with each project in Section Four to help you understand this concept. Begin with the straight-line stitching to stabilize the quilt during the rest of the process. Determine the centermost straight line and start with that line at the top of the quilt.

Now there is less bulk to deal with on either side. Once the center area is quilted, lay the quilt on the floor again. Carefully tape or T-pin the right side backing and fit the batting back exactly

Packaging the Quilt

To have good control of the quilt, it must be packaged properly. Lay the quilt in a large enough area to spread it flat. Roll it evenly from each side so the rolls are a few inches from your first quilting line (fig. 3–8). For a big quilt, once both sides have been rolled, I roll the bottom as well to make it easier to carry to the sewing machine (fig. 3–9).

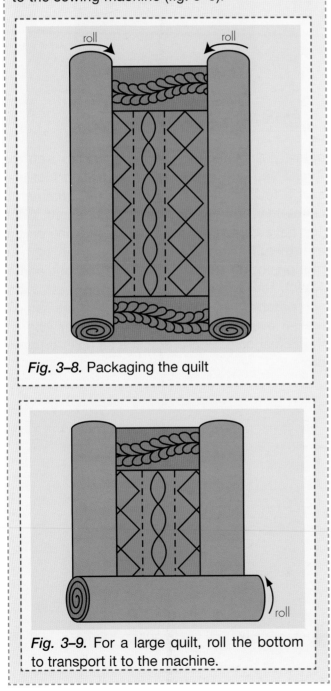

Fig. 3–8. Packaging the quilt

Fig. 3–9. For a large quilt, roll the bottom to transport it to the machine.

From the top of the quilt, sew the first straight line. Then, sew the next straight line directly to the right of the first line. The bulk of the quilt always moves to the left. The most there will ever be in the arm of the machine is half of the quilt or less. This makes managing a large quilt possible. This is why borders are the easiest to sew because there is nothing in the arm of machine.

Once all the rows are sewn to the right, turn the quilt 180 degrees, or upside down. Repackage the quilt to start with the next centermost line, sewing from the top down. Keep working to the right. Once you are done in this direction, turn the quilt a quarter turn and repackage to start with the centermost row and sew from the top down. Then continue to work to the right until all straight lines are complete in that direction. Next, turn the quilt 180 degrees and find the next centermost row. Continue to the right until all straight lines are machine quilted (fig. 3–10).

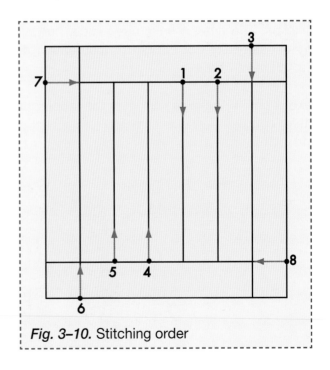

Fig. 3–10. Stitching order

Once the straight lines are complete, begin the designs that require free-motion quilting. Work in the order previously described. Find the center-most row of free-motion designs and package the quilt to sew from the top to the bottom. Work to the right and finish with the right border. Repackage and turn the quilt in the same order as figure 3–10, page 81, to complete the free-motion stitching on the quilt and borders.

The order of quilting each quilt is different. Some quilts need to be packaged on the diagonal, if that is how the straight lines and designs are positioned. Free-motion stitch designs such as feathers first before stipple quilting around them. The same goes for outlining, crosshatching, or diagonal lines. Also, sew one border at a time. If there is a continuous design that travels around all four borders, start at the top and stop at the bottom of each side keeping the bulk to the left. Then repackage, even on small quilts, to sew the next border, and so on.

I don't use clips to hold the rolls of the quilt package because my cotton or cotton-blend battings stay packaged nicely. If you use polyester batting, it may be helpful to use bicycle clips or banana hair clips. The times I have used clips, however, they occasionally got caught on something and caused uneven stitching.

Make a small package of the exact fabrics and batting you will use in a particular project (photo 3–11). Before starting the straight lines on the

Photo 3–11. Small quilt packages

actual quilt, thread the top and bobbin with the thread you will use. Attach the walking foot and sew a few practice rows of straight stitches to check tensions, threads, and stitch length. Once you have completed the straight stitching on the actual quilt and are ready to switch to free motion, bring this practice sample out again. Attach the darning foot, lower the feed dogs, and practice free-motion stitching on the sample first. If everything looks good, begin sewing on the actual quilt. I do a practice sample for every project.

Fig. 3–11. Supporting the quilt

Repackaging

There is a perception that it is hard to machine quilt on the home sewing machine because of the bulk of the quilt. I don't think this is true at all if the bulk is managed properly. Once you are in control of the quilt, the problems are minimal and you can achieve smooth, even stitches at all times. Repackaging allows me to get up from the machine every half hour or so to stretch. The sewing room information on page 24 is important and would be helpful to read again now that you have a better understanding of the quilt package.

You can freely and easily move a large project by packaging it properly, repackaging often, and keeping it supported all the time (fig. 3–11, page 82). Rest the quilt on your chest or over your shoulder to keep it from getting caught in your lap, which would cause it to stop moving freely. Stay as close to the machine as possible to keep the quilt from dropping into your lap. Whenever I can't move the quilt easily, it is time to reposition. It should feel like working on a 12" sample square, even with a large project. If you don't feel that way, reposition your fingers and/or the quilt itself to allow more free movement.

Rolling the quilt on either side of the area you are sewing controls the backing fabric. You can't see the back of the quilt while sewing, but rolling keeps the backing flat and controlled. You can see the top and control any fullness. With a well-basted quilt and packaging in this fashion, you won't get puckers or folds of fabric on the back. There are other approaches that work as well. Some quilters puddle the quilt instead of rolling it. If you have room to do this, it can work well.

Once you are confident that you can manage the quilt, you have won the battle! With these techniques, you are always in control and can happily manage even the biggest quilts. Plan the order of the quilting first then package properly. You now have all the information needed to complete the machine quilting of your project.

Finishing
Binding

The most exciting part about making the binding is that your quilt is almost finished. As with everything else, there are many ways to bind. There are great books that cover this subject in depth and offer a variety of choices. For my traditional quilts, I do not prefer a completely machine-made binding. I mainly use either a straight or bias double binding. The binding is sewn to the quilt top first with the walking foot and straight stitch on the sewing machine. Miter the corners of the binding as you sew. Bring the binding to the back of the quilt and hand stitch it to the backing. It is possible to sew this by machine. I have also used a single binding on some quilts.

With machine quilting, it is easy to have a little distortion along the edge of the quilt. This is controlled in the binding phase (see sidebar). The first step to binding is to lay the quilt flat and measure to see if it is even. Next, square the quilt by cutting off the excess backing and batting used during quilting. Be careful to not trim away too much. The backing and batting should fill the binding completely and if too much of it is trimmed, it can't be replaced. I use a quilters' ruler, quilters' square, matboard, and rotary cutter to trim the excess accurately, allowing all four corners to be completely square.

Correcting Distortion

Minor discrepancies found when measuring can be corrected by pressing lightly once the excess backing and batting is trimmed. I rarely have major discrepancies. If the edge has any noticeable distortion, press very lightly with an iron to correct. I am careful when using an iron on my quilted quilts and always use a pressing cloth. I only do this if there is noticeable distortion and rarely have to resort to this step. If your quilt is evenly quilted, you will be less likely to have distortion along the edges. If you find major problems, you may need to quilt a little more to even things out.

A small quilt can be placed directly on a large mat-board to use the ruler and rotary cutter to trim the outside edge. Place a large quilt on the floor and, after measuring to see if it is evenly laid out, place the matboard on the floor under the quilt to trim the outside edge. It is well worth taking your time with this step. The thread basting, which is about ¼" from the edge of the quilt top, can be used as a guide to trim to about ½" away from the basting. This gives you room to square the quilt and keep the size consistent. Some of this may eventually be trimmed away for a narrower binding after the binding is sewn to the top of the quilt.

Straight Versus Bias Binding

I have used both bias and straight bindings on my quilts. I usually use a bias binding for bed quilts or quilts that will get a lot of use. This is because the edge of binding that receives the wear is folded along the bias and has more threads to handle the wear. Straight binding is folded along one or two threads and wears out more quickly. On antique quilts that have a straight binding, you can see this effect. For quilts that receive little use, straight binding is a fine choice. I use a bias binding if a check or plaid fabric is used because I like the look of these fabrics on the bias. Many times, I choose straight binding if there is a small amount of fabric left for the binding.

Figure the amount of binding by adding together the length of the four sides of the quilt plus 10". For example, if your quilt is 45" x 45", you need 190" of binding. If you use straight binding, you would need five strips cut from the crosswise grain of the yardage. If you use bias binding, you need to measure each strip to get the appropriate amount (fig. 3–12).

Double Binding

For large quilts, 2½" wide strips are generally used. For small quilts, 2¼" wide strips are used. With this 2¼" size binding, trim the backing and batting a little closer to ¼" from the basting on the

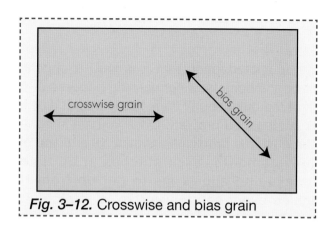
Fig. 3–12. Crosswise and bias grain

outer edge. Cut the strips the appropriate width and sew them together on the diagonal. Press the seams open, then press the entire binding in half. The binding is now ready to be sewn to the quilt.

Package the quilt just like when machine quilting, with the bulk to the left of the machine. On your sewing machine, use thread that matches the color of the binding, a straight stitch, and a walk-ing-foot attachment. Leave about 5" of the binding loose and start sewing along one side of the quilt, about one quarter of the way from the quilt top. Sew an accurate ¼" seam allowance, follow-ing the edge of the quilt as a guide. I do not pin the binding before sewing it to the quilt because the walking foot helps guide the binding evenly. The binding should fit snugly. As you sew, lay the binding smoothly and with a little tautness along the edge of the quilt. Holding the binding firmly while sewing keeps it flat and smooth.

To miter the corners, place a pin at the ¼" point from the end of the quilt. Sew to this point and backstitch a few stitches. End the stitching and fold the binding back at a 90-degree angle, fold the binding back again to align with the next side of the quilt (fig. 3–13, page 85). Repackage the bulk. Continue to sew from the edge of the quilt, mitering the remaining corners. End the stitching, leaving about 4" between ends. Measure carefully and piece these ends on the diagonal. Press the seam allowance open. Finish sewing the final 4" of binding by machine. Turn the folded edge to the back and carefully hand stitch it around the quilt. Neatly miter corners and sew the miters (fig. 3–14, page 85).

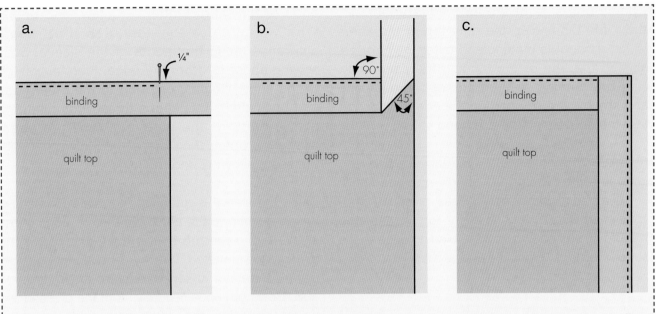

Fig. 3–13. Mitering the corners: **(a)** Sew until reaching the ¼" mark at the pin. **(b)** Fold the binding back at a 90-degree angle. **(c)** Align the binding with the next side of the quilt.

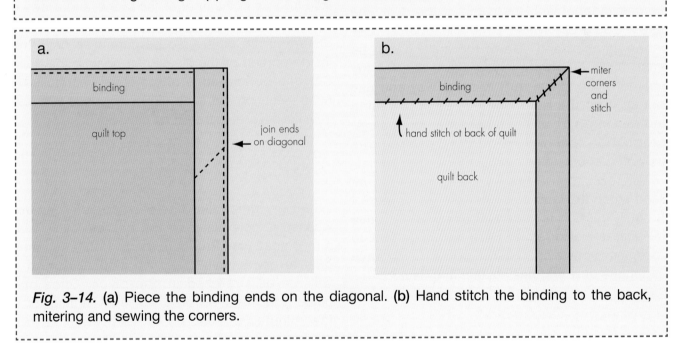

Fig. 3–14. **(a)** Piece the binding ends on the diagonal. **(b)** Hand stitch the binding to the back, mitering and sewing the corners.

It is possible to sew the binding to the back of the quilt on the machine. To do this, hand baste the folded edge of binding to the back, so the basting is beyond the first row of stitching. With nylon thread on the top of the machine, or matching cotton thread, stitch in the ditch from the top of the quilt. This looks neat from the front, but unless you hand baste carefully, the back can look messy. It is almost as easy to hand stitch.

Single Binding

The single binding is made almost the same as double binding. I have resorted to a single binding when I have a small amount of fabric. A 1¼" or 1½" wide strip of fabric is generally used for this binding. For the length of binding, refer to the guidelines for double binding, page 84. Sew the strips together on the diagonal. It is helpful to press one side of the long edge under ¼". Attach the binding to the quilt top in the same fashion as double binding and miter the corners, finishing the end of the binding the same way. Bring the binding to the back of the quilt and hand stitch, carefully turning the edge under ¼". Miter the corners neatly and hand stitch.

After binding, lay the quilt on the table or floor and make sure the binding fits snugly and lies flat. If there is a little distortion or waviness, press the binding carefully with a pressing cloth. You may need to measure again and even pin the binding edge to the floor or a board to block the quilt slightly.

Labeling

Always label your finished quilt. It can be a simple muslin label with the name of the quilt, the date it was made, your name, full address, telephone number, and size of the quilt. It can be much more elaborate if you like. I like for my label to relate to the quilt in some way and use fabrics from the quilt, sometimes appliquéing and piecing part of the label. You can include information that will help future generations know and appreciate your quilt.

Hand stitch the label to the lower right corner of the quilt back. It is important to do this in case the quilt is lost or stolen. It is also important to document your work. Isn't it wonderful to have an antique quilt that has a name and date?

Making a Sleeve

You may want to display your quilt on the wall or enter it in quilt shows that require a sleeve on the back. If you enter it in a show, read the rules for proper placement and size of the sleeve. I use a tube for my sleeves and hand stitch them to the back of the quilt at the top.

Measure the quilt width and subtract 1". Cut the sleeve fabric this length by 8½" wide. If it is a small wall quilt, the width could be 2½". Fold the

ends of the fabric under ¼", sew, and press. With wrong sides together, sew a ¼" seam allowance along the length of the sleeve. Start sewing about ½" from the edge, then backstitch to the edge. Continue sewing to the other edge and backstitch. This keeps thread from showing at the ends of the sleeve. Press the seam allowance open, then press the sleeve flat with the seam allowance to the middle.

When the sleeve is attached, no raw edges show. With the seam to the back, pin the top edge of the sleeve along the top of the quilt, just below the binding and centered. Sew by hand along the edge, being careful not to sew through to the front of the quilt. Sew both ends securely. With the pressed line on the bottom of the sleeve as a guide, bring the edge up about ¼" and pin in place. This achieves a little fullness in the front of the sleeve and allows a dowel or tube to be placed in the sleeve without distorting the quilt. Also be careful to have the inside portion of the sleeve flat against the quilt. Sew the bottom edge of the sleeve carefully by hand, securing the ends (fig. 3–15, page 87). You now have a usable sleeve for hanging.

Care of Your Quilt

I treat my quilts like fine washables. They are washed in cold water on the delicate cycle with a mild soap (see Products, page 110). I hang my quilt to dry, usually over two clotheslines so it will not be stretched in one place. Once dry, place it in the dryer on a low-heat setting for a few minutes to fluff. Try to keep washing to a minimum. I wash my fabric in the same mild soap that is used to wash my quilts, and pre-treat my cotton-blend batting before use. I like to know exactly what is going to happen to my quilt before washing. If you use nylon thread, be careful to not iron the thread or use a very hot dryer, because it is slightly heat sensitive.

Store your quilts carefully. If my quilts are not on a bed or on the wall, I roll them around plastic PVC pipes. I try not to keep my quilts folded

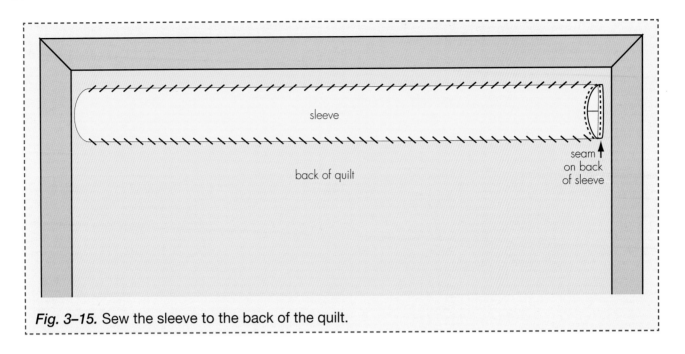

Fig. 3–15. Sew the sleeve to the back of the quilt.

over long periods of time. After spending a lot of time, energy, and expense on your quilts, you want to take good care of them.

I have enjoyed sharing my approach to machine quilting with you. If you are just beginning to explore machine quilting, this is a good starting point. If you have more experience, I hope that some of my ideas will improve your skills and help you enjoy quilting. Whether you want to quilt quickly with simple designs or more elaborately, you can be successful without a struggle. I truly enjoy machine quilting even large quilts. Please try one or more of the practice projects in the next section to apply these skills in an actual project. You will then be ready to move on to your own quilts!

PROJECTS

AMISH BARS

Finished size: 28" x 28"

Photo 4–1. AMISH BARS, by the author. Enjoy exploring all the basic concepts of machine quilting, including straight lines, stipple quilting, and marked designs on this small project. Cotton fabric, thread, and cotton-blend batting were used.

Requirements

Pre-washed and pressed 100 percent cotton fabric was used. Yardage is based on a 40" width of fabric.

Fabric	¾ yard blue ¾ yard pink (binding included)
Backing	1 yard print to coordinate with top fabrics
Batting	32" x 32" cotton or cotton blend
Thread	Two 164-yard spools blue, 50-weight cotton Two 164-yard spools pink, 50-weight cotton or One spool invisible thread for top Two 164-yard spools 50-weight cotton to match backing for bobbin
Needle	80/12 Microtex for 50-weight cotton thread or 70/10 Microtex for invisible thread

Cutting

Quilt top	Six 20½" x 4½" blue strips Three 20½" x 4½" pink strips Four 4½" pink squares
Backing	32" x 32"

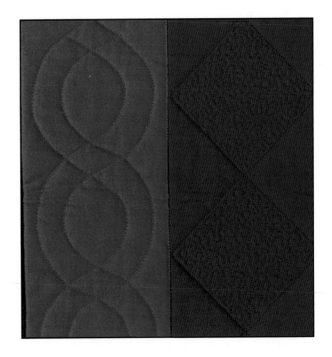

Technique Primer

Marking .... p. 75
Basting .... p. 77
Stipple Quilting .... p. 34
Marked Designs, Cable .... p. 56
Feathers .... p. 57
Double Binding .... p. 84

Construction

1. With an accurate ¼" seam allowance, piece the quilt top according to figure 4–1. Press the seam allowances toward the blue fabric. Press the entire quilt top.

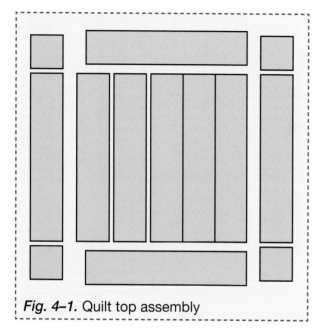

Fig. 4–1. Quilt top assembly

2. Mark the quilt top with feathers, cables, the square design, and the corner design on pages 100–103, referring to figure 4–2 for placement of these designs. Layer the quilt top, batting, and backing, and baste.

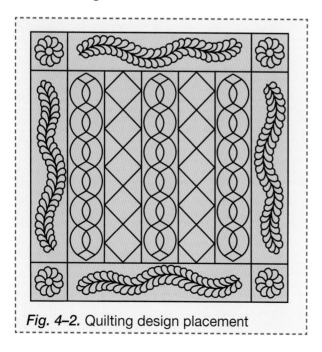

Fig. 4–2. Quilting design placement

3. Make a practice sample with fabrics from the quilt and batting. Thread the machine with the thread that you will use for this project. I started with pink thread for straight stitching in the ditch on the pink bars. Attach the walking foot and practice one row of straight stitching to check tensions, stitch length, and thread color.

4. Begin straight stitching in the order shown (fig. 4–3). Repackage the quilt properly with each turn. Once rows 1–8 are sewn, most of the straight stitching is complete.

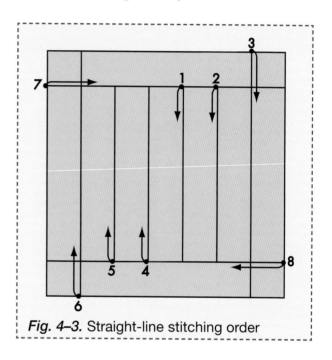

Fig. 4–3. Straight-line stitching order

5. The squares on point can be sewn with the walking foot or by free motion with the darning foot. If you use the walking foot, the squares are sewn by pivoting and turning the quilt slightly (fig. 4–4, page 91). This works on a small project.

6. To free-motion quilt, attach the darning foot and lower the feed dogs. Sew the designs that use pink thread first. Practice free-motion stitching on the sample to warm up and check tensions and thread choice. Free-motion quilt in the order shown (fig. 4–5, page 91), sewing the cables and the feather wreaths in the corners. Repackage the quilt with each turn.

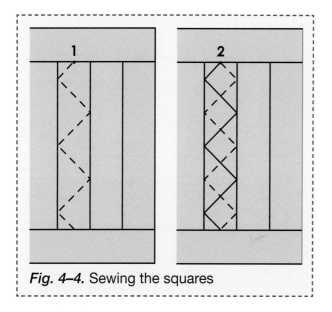

Fig. 4–4. Sewing the squares

Please note if you use nylon thread, you do not have to go through the order two times. Just start at the centermost design and work to the right to complete every design.

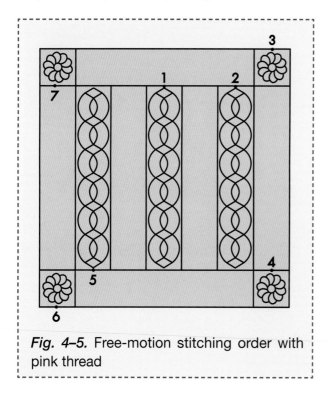

Fig. 4–5. Free-motion stitching order with pink thread

ing in the squares on point, starting at the top square and working down. Keep this continuous by sneaking through where squares on point touch. Repackage the quilt with each turn.

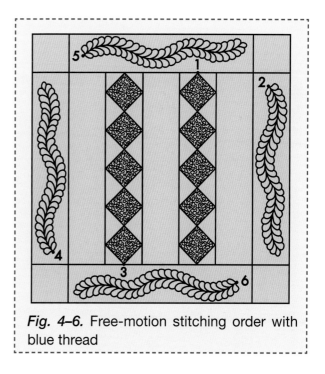

Fig. 4–6. Free-motion stitching order with blue thread

8. Bind the quilt with a 2½" wide straight double binding of pink fabric.

7. Change to blue thread in the top and bobbin. Practice free-motion stitching on the small sample with blue thread, checking tensions and thread choice. Free-motion quilt in the order shown (fig. 4–6). Begin by stipple quilt-

No-Mark Sampler

Finished size: 25" x 25"

Photo 4–2. No-mark Sampler, by the author. You can have fun exploring no-mark designs on this small, easy-to-manage quilt. Cotton fabric, cotton and rayon thread, and cotton-blend batting were used.

Requirements

Pre-washed and pressed 100 percent cotton fabric was used. Yardage is based on a 40" width of fabric.

Fabric	⅓ yard orange ½ yard purple (binding included) ⅓ yard pink
Backing	1 yard print to coordinate with top fabrics
Batting	29" x 29" cotton or cotton blend
Thread	Two 164-yard spools orange 50-weight cotton One 164-yard spool purple 50-weight cotton One 164-yard spool pink 50-weight cotton One spool decorative thread (variegated rayon)
Needles	80/12 Microtex for 50-weight cotton thread Appropriate needle for decorative thread

Cutting

Blocks	Five 7½" orange squares Four 7½" purple squares
Sashing and Borders*	Six 1½" x 7½" pink strips Four 1½" x 23½" pink strips Two 1½" x 25½" pink strips
Backing	29" x 29"

*Measure the quilt top in progress for accuracy.

Technique Primer

Marking......................................p. 75
Basting ....p. 77
No-mark Variations....................p. 36
Double Binding..........................p. 84

𝒞onstruction

1. With an accurate ¼" seam allowance, piece the quilt top according to figure 4–7. Press the seam allowances toward the pink sashing. Press the entire quilt top.

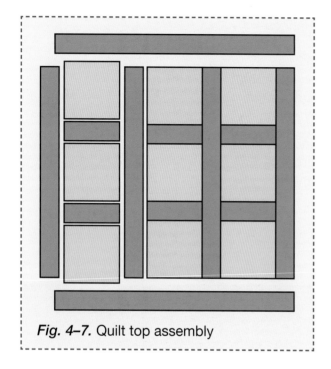

Fig. 4–7. Quilt top assembly

2. Mark a 1" grid on the center orange block for curvy crosshatching. Mark the heart on page 95 in the lower left orange block. Layer the quilt top, batting, and backing, and baste.

3. Make a practice sample with fabrics from the quilt and batting. Thread the machine with the thread that you will use for the straight lines on this project. Attach the walking foot and practice one row of straight stitching on the sample to check tensions, stitch length, and thread color.

4. Begin straight stitching in the ditch on your quilt in the order shown (fig. 4–8). Remember to repackage the quilt properly with each turn. Once rows 1–12 are sewn, the straight stitching is complete.

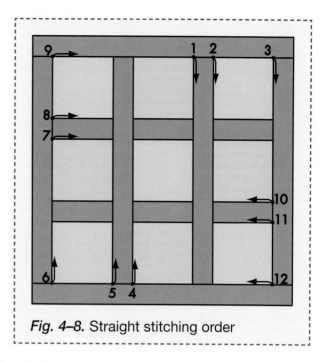

Fig. 4–8. Straight stitching order

5. Switch to free-motion quilting. Attach the darning foot and lower the feed dogs. Thread the machine with the thread that will be used next on the quilt. I used pink thread in the top and bobbin first. Practice free-motion quilting on your sample square to warm up and check tensions and thread color. Refer to figure 4–9, page 95, for placement of designs in each square.

6. Practice each variation on the sample square, then sew on the quilt. Package properly and work so the bulk of the quilt is to the left. Use the order described in figure 4–8 as a guide. Sew the sashing first with a loopy meandering design. Next, sew the curvy crosshatching in the center orange square. Switch to orange thread in the top and bobbin and sew the four outer orange squares. Switch to decorative thread in the top and cotton thread in the bobbin to sew the purple squares, changing the needle if needed. Practice on the sample square, checking tensions with decorative threads. With the 40-weight variegated rayon thread, I needed to loosen my top tension and used a 90/14 needle.

7. Bind the quilt with a 2¼" wide straight double binding of purple fabric.

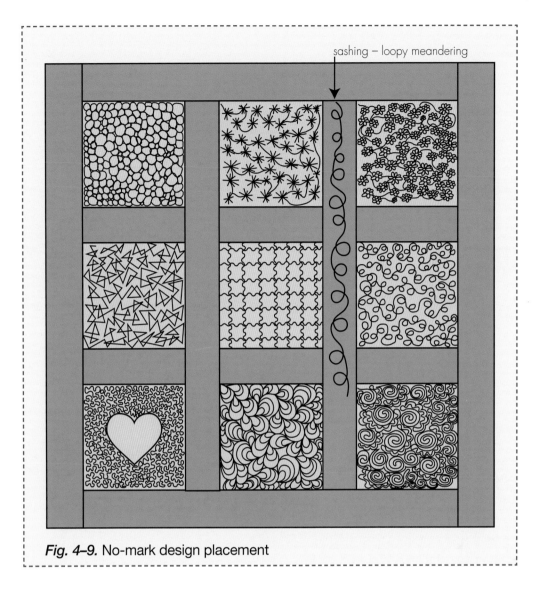

sashing – loopy meandering

Fig. 4–9. No-mark design placement

FEATHER SAMPLER

Finished size 27" x 27"

Photo 4–3. FEATHER SAMPLER, by the author. Explore traditional ideas for machine quilting, such as feathers and stipple quilting, on this small, easy–to–manage quilt. Cotton fabric, thread, and cotton-blend batting were used.

Requirements

Pre-washed and pressed 100 percent cotton fabric was used. Yardage is based on a 40" width of fabric.

Fabric	1 yard cream
	1¼ yards red-cream print (backing included)
	¼ yard each of one solid red and two assorted red prints or ¼ yard red print for solid sashing instead of Sawtooth border
Binding	⅓ yard red print
Batting	31" x 31" cotton or cotton blend
Thread	Three 164-yard spools cream 50-weight cotton One 164-yard spool red 50-weight cotton or Invisible thread on top and two spools 50-weight cotton in bobbin
Needle	80/12 Microtex for 50 weight cotton thread or 70/10 Microtex for invisible thread

Cutting

Blocks	Four 8½" cream squares
Borders*	Four 4½" x 19½" cream strips Four 4½" red-cream print squares
Sashing	Four 1½" x 8½" red-cream print strips One 1½" red print square
Sawtooth†	Sixty-eight 1⅞" assorted red, red print, and red-cream print squares Four 1½" red squares
Backing	31" x 31"

*Measure the quilt in progress for accuracy.
†If you prefer, you can substitute the Sawtooth border with four 1½" x 17½" red print strips.

Technique Primer

Marking .... p. 75
Basting .... p. 77
Feathers .... p. 57
Stipple Quilting .... p. 34
Double Binding .... p. 84

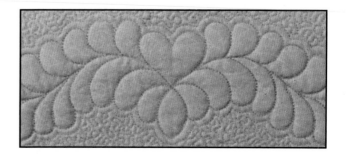

Construction

1. Place a red 1⅞" square and a red print 1⅞" square right sides together. Draw a diagonal line on the print square and sew ¼" away from the line on each side. Cut on the diagonal line and press the two half-squares open. Make sixty-eight 1½" half-square units (fig. 4–10). Make four borders by joining 17 half-square units for each border.

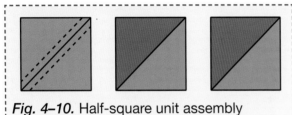

Fig. 4–10. Half-square unit assembly

2. With an accurate ¼" seam allowance, piece the quilt top according to figure 4–11. Press the seam allowances toward the blocks and borders. If you are using strips instead of saw-tooth sashing, press the seam allowances toward the strips. Press the entire quilt top.

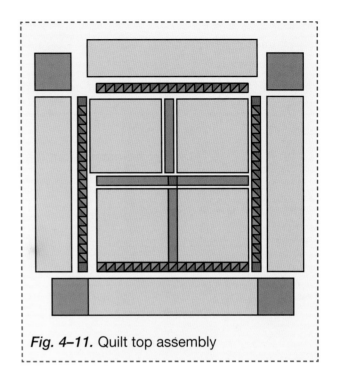

Fig. 4–11. Quilt top assembly

3. Mark the quilt top with the feather designs on pages 104–108, referring to figure 4–12 for placement of these designs. Layer the quilt top, batting, and backing, and baste.

Fig. 4–12. Feather placement

4. Make a practice sample with the fabrics from the quilt top and batting. Mark a portion of a feather on this sample. Thread the machine with light-colored cotton thread in the top and bobbin, or with invisible thread in the top and cotton thread in the bobbin.

5. Attach the walking foot and practice one row of straight stitching on the sample to check tensions, stitch length, and thread color. Begin straight stitching in the ditch on your quilt in the order shown (fig. 4–13). Repackage the quilt properly with each turn. Once rows 1–12 are sewn, the straight stitching is complete.

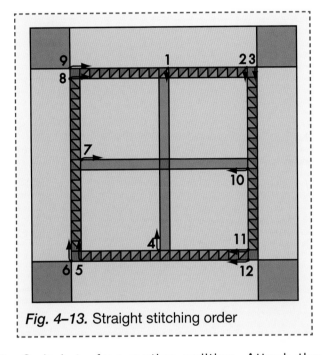

Fig. 4–13. Straight stitching order

6. Switch to free-motion quilting. Attach the darning foot and lower the feed dogs. Practice on the sample to warm up and check tensions and thread color. Package the quilt properly and sew in the order shown (fig. 4–14). If the stitching order for the feather is different from the traditional order, it is indicated on the pattern page. Sew the feather design in one section, traditional stipple quilt around the design, then move to the next section. Repackage the quilt with each turn. If you would like to use a finer thread for the stipple quilting, change thread after all the feathers are sewn, then stipple quilt in the

same order. You can also outline all the feathers after they are sewn using your darning foot as a guide.

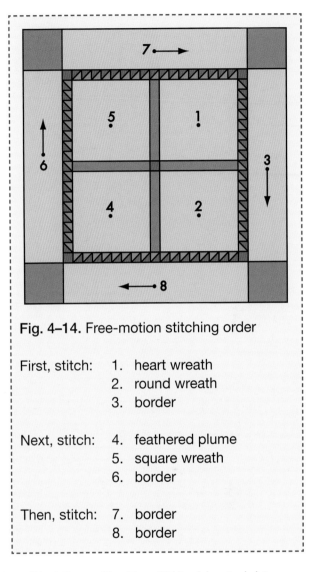

Fig. 4–14. Free-motion stitching order

First, stitch: 1. heart wreath
　　　　　　　　2. round wreath
　　　　　　　　3. border

Next, stitch: 4. feathered plume
　　　　　　　　5. square wreath
　　　　　　　　6. border

Then, stitch: 7. border
　　　　　　　　8. border

7. Bind the quilt with a 2½" wide straight double binding of red fabric.

AMISH BARS

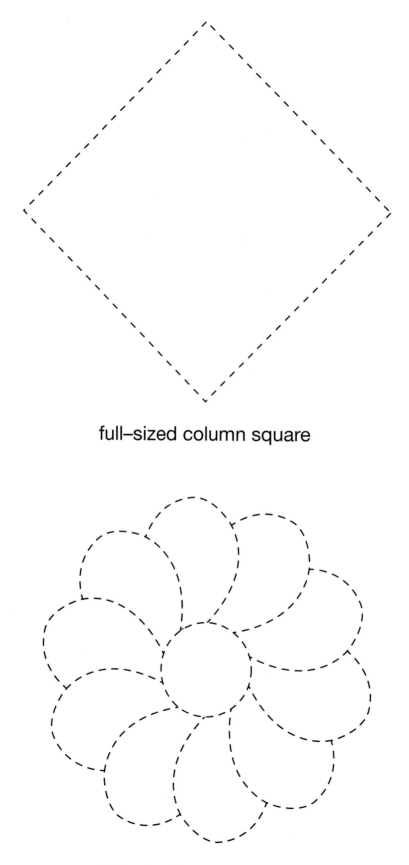

full–sized column square

full–sized corner pattern

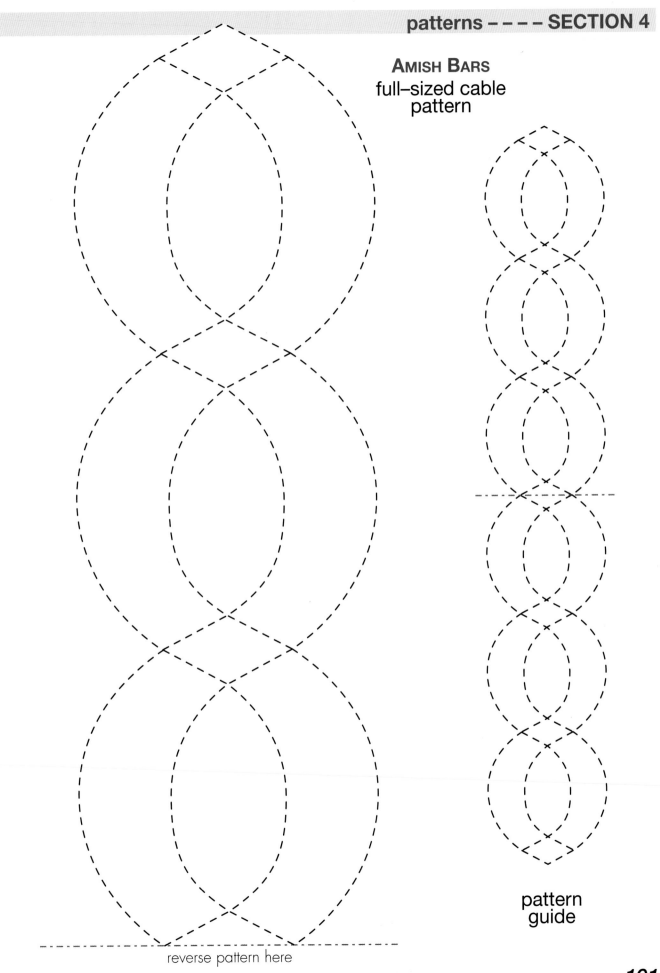

AMISH BARS
full–sized cable
pattern

pattern
guide

reverse pattern here

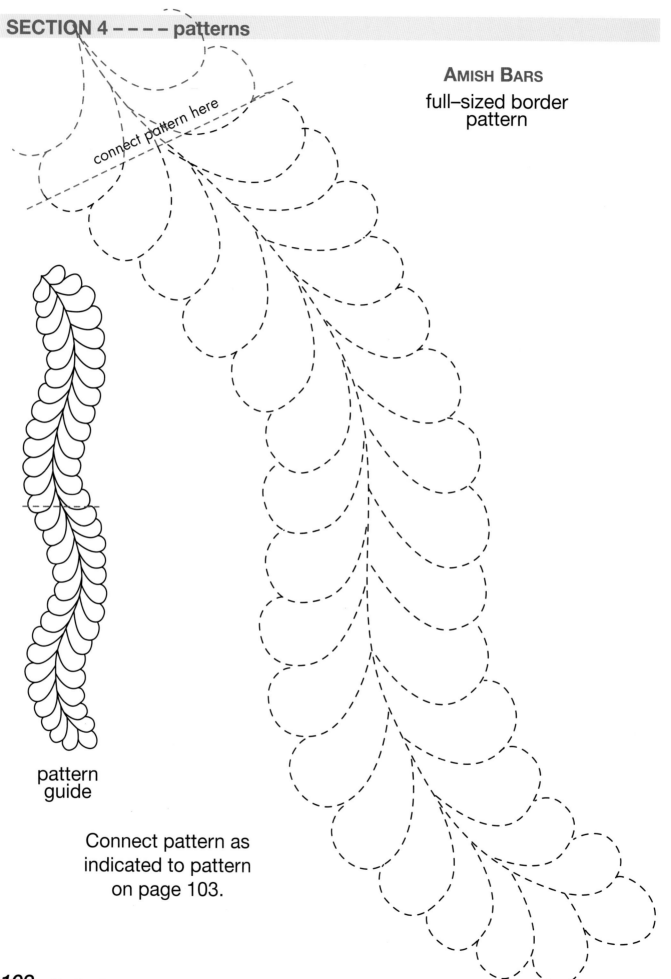

AMISH BARS
full–sized border
pattern

connect pattern here

pattern
guide

Connect pattern as
indicated to pattern
on page 103.

AMISH BARS

full–sized border
pattern

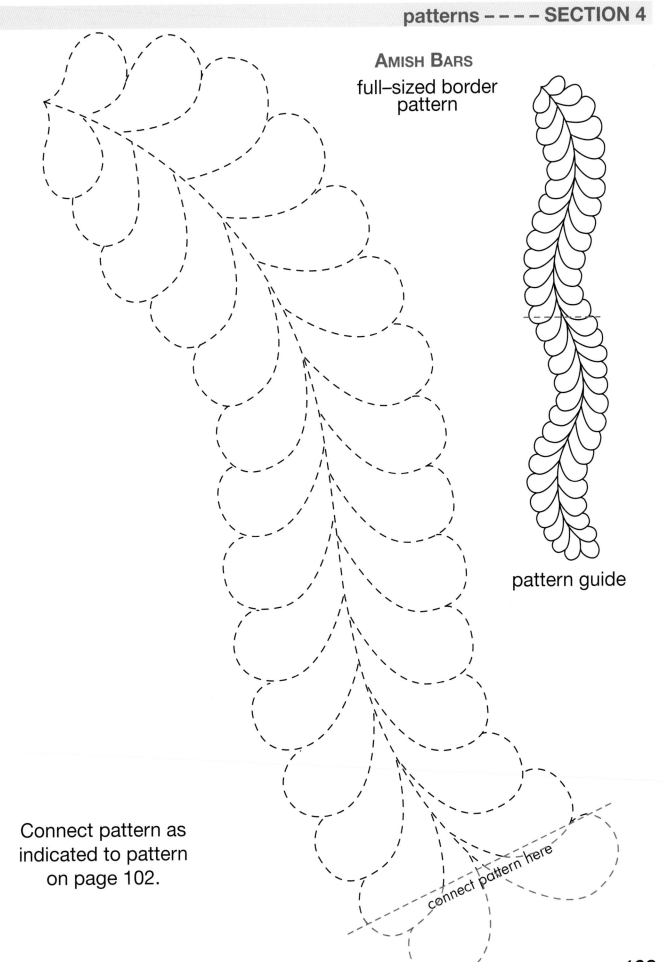

pattern guide

Connect pattern as
indicated to pattern
on page 102.

connect pattern here

FEATHER SAMPLER

Stitching Order

1. Sew the right center spine.
2. Sew the right inside feathers.
3. Sew the right outside feathers, then repeat steps 1–3 for the left side.

HEART WREATH
full–sized pattern

FEATHER SAMPLER

full–sized round wreath pattern

FEATHER SAMPLER

Stitching Order

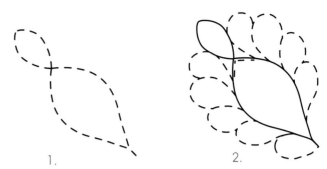

1.
2.

full–sized
feathered plume pattern

full–sized
square wreath pattern

Refer to page 63 for instructions on the plume feather when sewing the outside feathers.

FEATHER SAMPLER

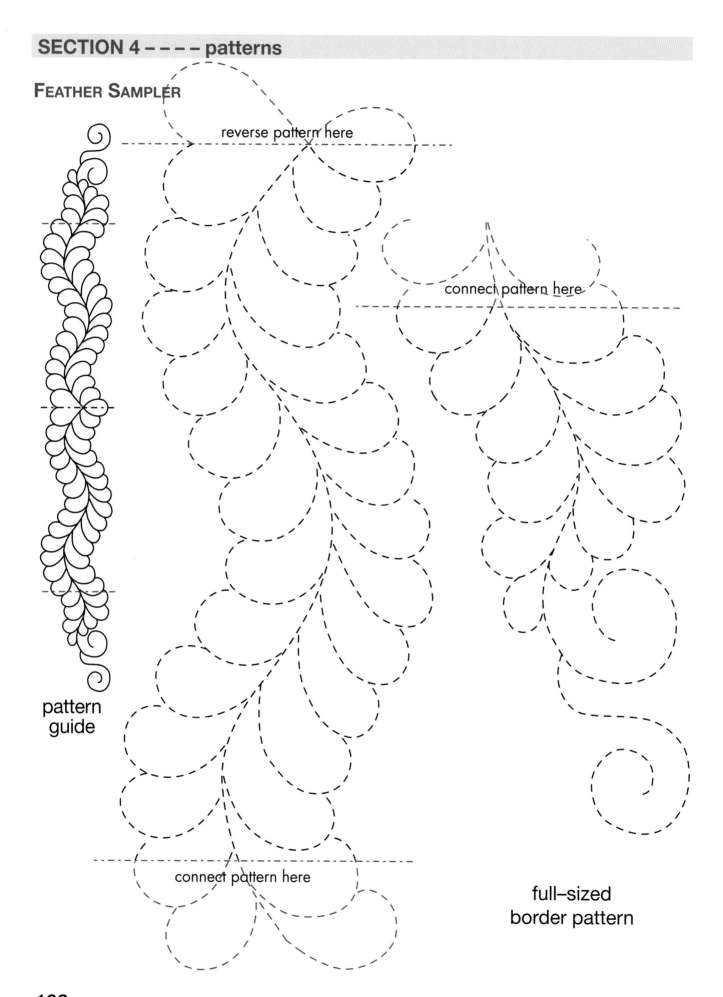

reverse pattern here

connect pattern here

pattern
guide

connect pattern here

full–sized
border pattern

BIBLIOGRAPHY

These books are wonderful sources for information on machine quilting and the sewing machine.

Fanning, Robbie and Tony. *The Complete Book of Machine Quilting*. Radnor, Pennsylvania: Chilton Needlework, 1980.

Frager, Dorothy. *The Quilting Primer*. Radnor, Pennsylvania: Chilton Needlework, 1979.

Garbers, Debbie and Janet F. O'Brien. *Point Well Taken: The Guide to Success with Needles & Threads*. Marietta, Georgia: An In Cahoots Book, 1996.

Hargrave, Harriet. *Heirloom Machine Quilting*. Lafayette, California: C&T Publishing, 1990.

Holly, Pat and Sue Nickels. *Amish Patterns for Machine Quilting*. Mineola, New York: Dover Publications, Inc., 1997.

Holly, Pat and Sue Nickels. *60 Machine Quilting Patterns*. Mineola, New York: Dover Publications, 1994.

Kolb, Alice. *Sew Crazy with Decorative Threads and Stitches*. Paducah, Kentucky: American Quilter's Society, 2002.

Lehman, Libby. *Threadplay – Mastering Machine Embroidery Techniques*. Bothell, Washington: That Patchwork Place, 1997.

Marston, Gwen and Joe Cunningham. *Quilting with Style: Principles for Great Pattern Design*. Paducah, Kentucky: American Quilter's Society, 1993.

Meyer, Suellen. "The Sewing Machine and Visible Machine Stitching on Nineteenth-Century Quilts." In *Quiltmaking in America: Beyond the Myths, selected writings from the American Quilt Study Group*, edited by Laurel Horton. Nashville, Tennessee: Rutledge Hill Press, 1994.

Wagner, Debra. *Teach Yourself Machine Piecing and Quilting*. Radnor, Pennsylvania: Chilton Book Company, 1992.

YLI Corporation Brochure: *The Thread of Truth – A Factual Look at Sewing Thread*. YLI Corporation, www.ylicorp.com.

PRODUCTS

I have researched these products and am confident of the success achieved with them. There are other products that work well, but these are the ones I have found that work the best with the techniques being used. Most of the products are available at quilt shops.

100 percent cotton batting: Hobbs, Fairfield, Mountain Mist®, and Warm and Natural®

Adjustable lamp: Ott-Lite®

Cotton-blend batting: Hobbs Heirloom® 80/20 blend

Cotton thread (50-weight/2-ply): Madeira Tanne

Mercerized cotton thread (50-weight/3-ply): Mettler® Silk Finish

Mild soap: Orvus® Paste

Safety pin closer: Kwik Klip

Silver marking pencil: Roxanne's Quilter's Choice

Wholecloth stencil for FEATHER/CABLE MINI SAMPLER: Quilting Creations International, Inc.

To contact Sue, visit her website at www.Sue.Nickels.com.

With a passion for precision, Sue Nickels has mastered the art of machine quilt-making. She has taught for guilds and at conferences and quilt shows around the country, as well as in England. Her machine-quilted quilts have won many awards, including the 1998 AQS Best of Show. Sue has co-authored two books with her sister, Pat Holly, on machine-quilting patterns. She also designs stencils for Quilting Creations International, Inc. Living in Michigan with her husband and two daughters, Sue enjoys sharing her skills on machine techniques with quilters everywhere and will continue making machine-quilted quilts in a traditional way.

Other AQS Books

This is only a small selection of the books available from the American Quilter's Society. AQS books are known worldwide for timely topics, clear writing, beautiful color photos, and accurate illustrations and patterns. The following books are available from your local bookseller, quilt shop, or public library.

#6414   us$25.95

#6072   us$25.95

#6006   us$25.95

#6419 (12" x 9")   us$22.95

#5855   us$22.95

#6069 (12" x 9")   us$24.95

#6070   us$24.95

#6071   us$22.95

#6296   us$25.95